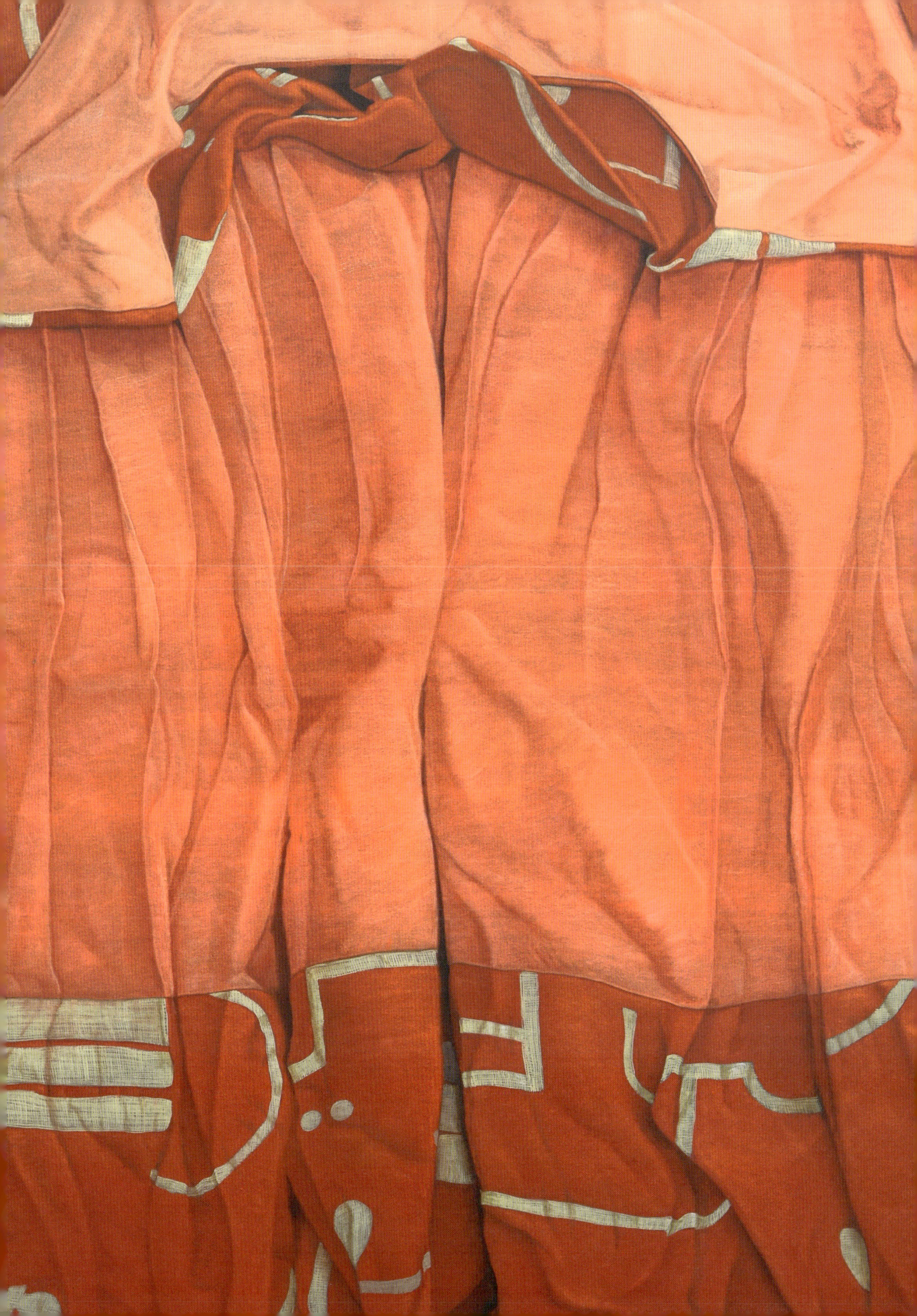

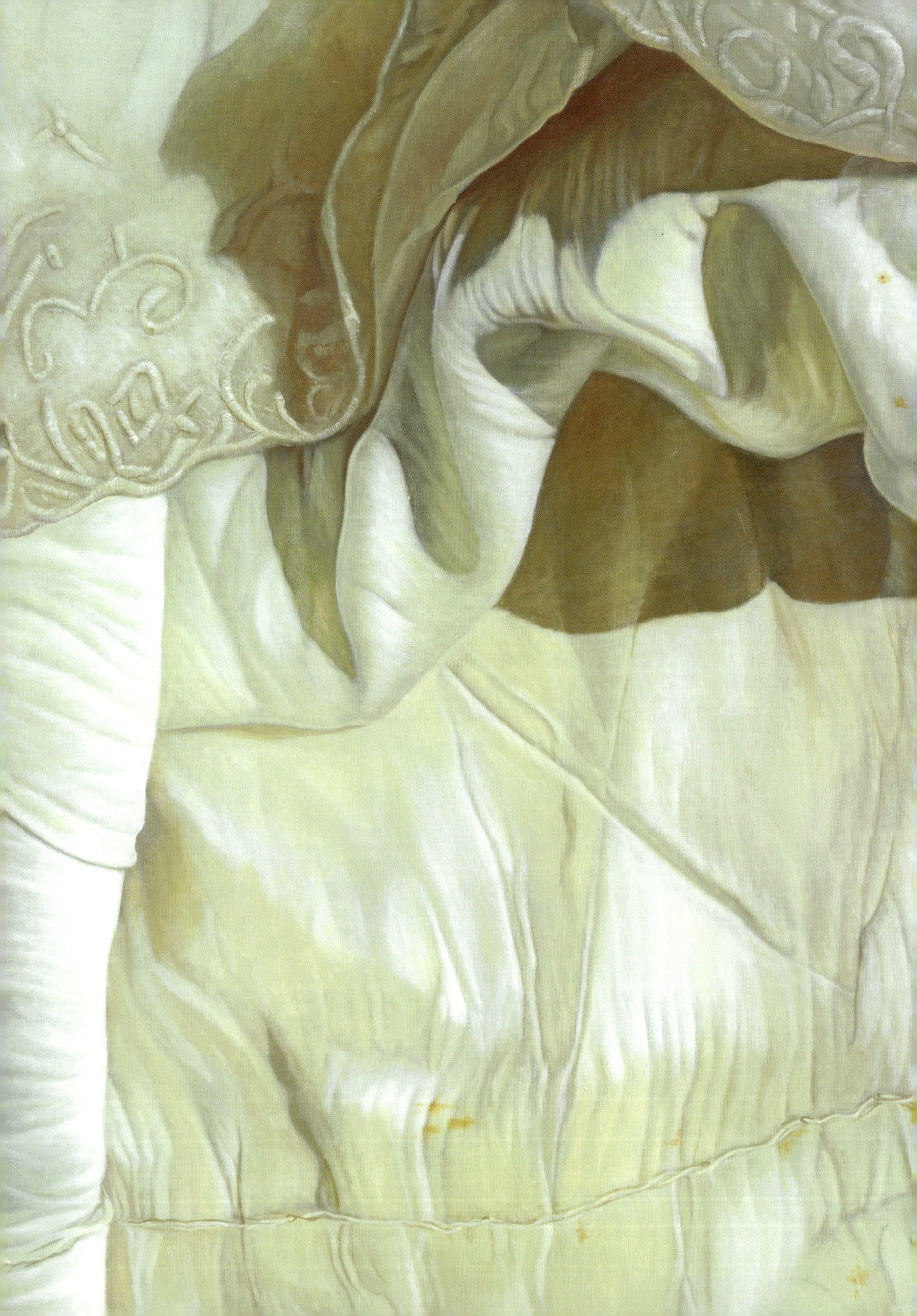

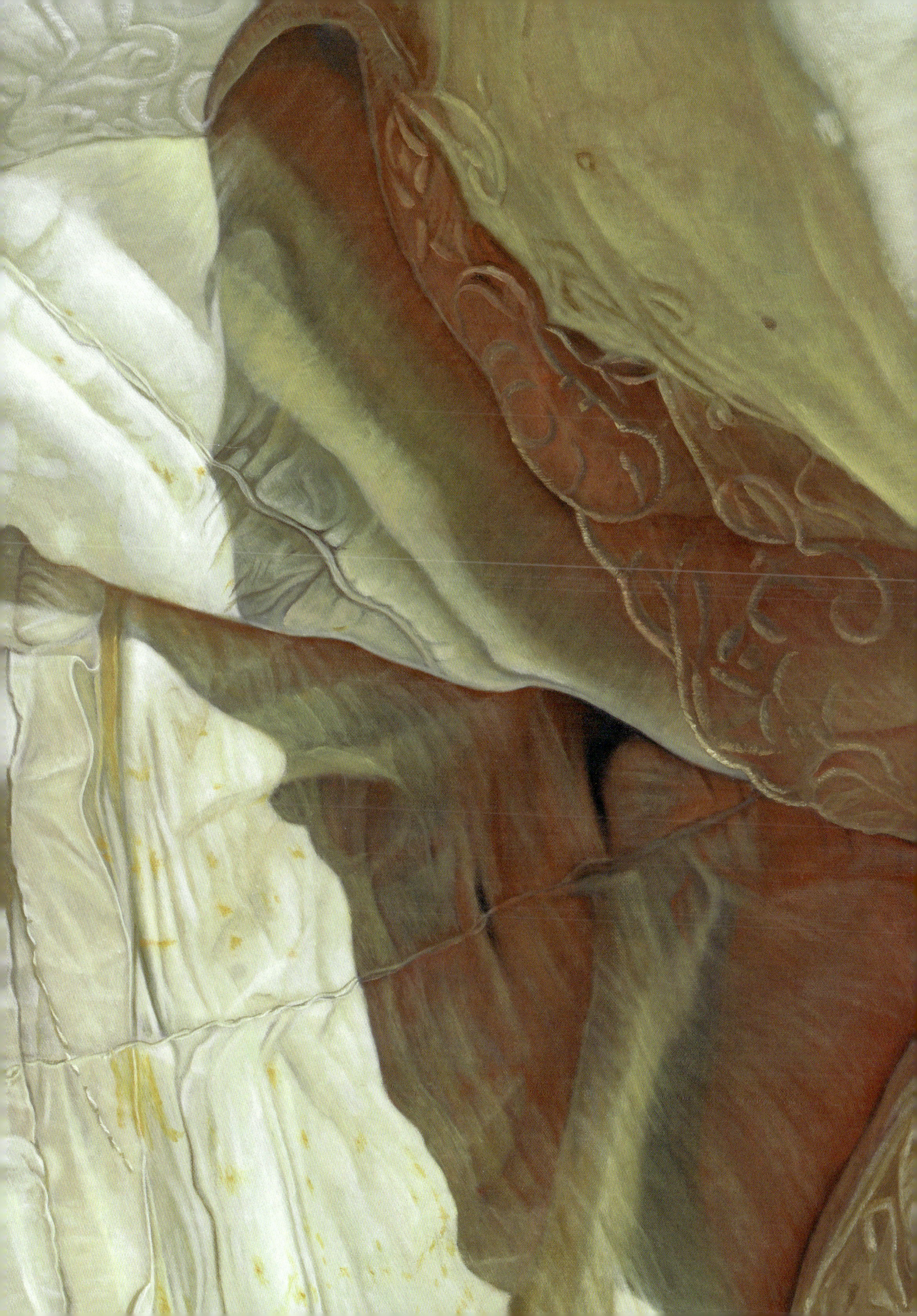

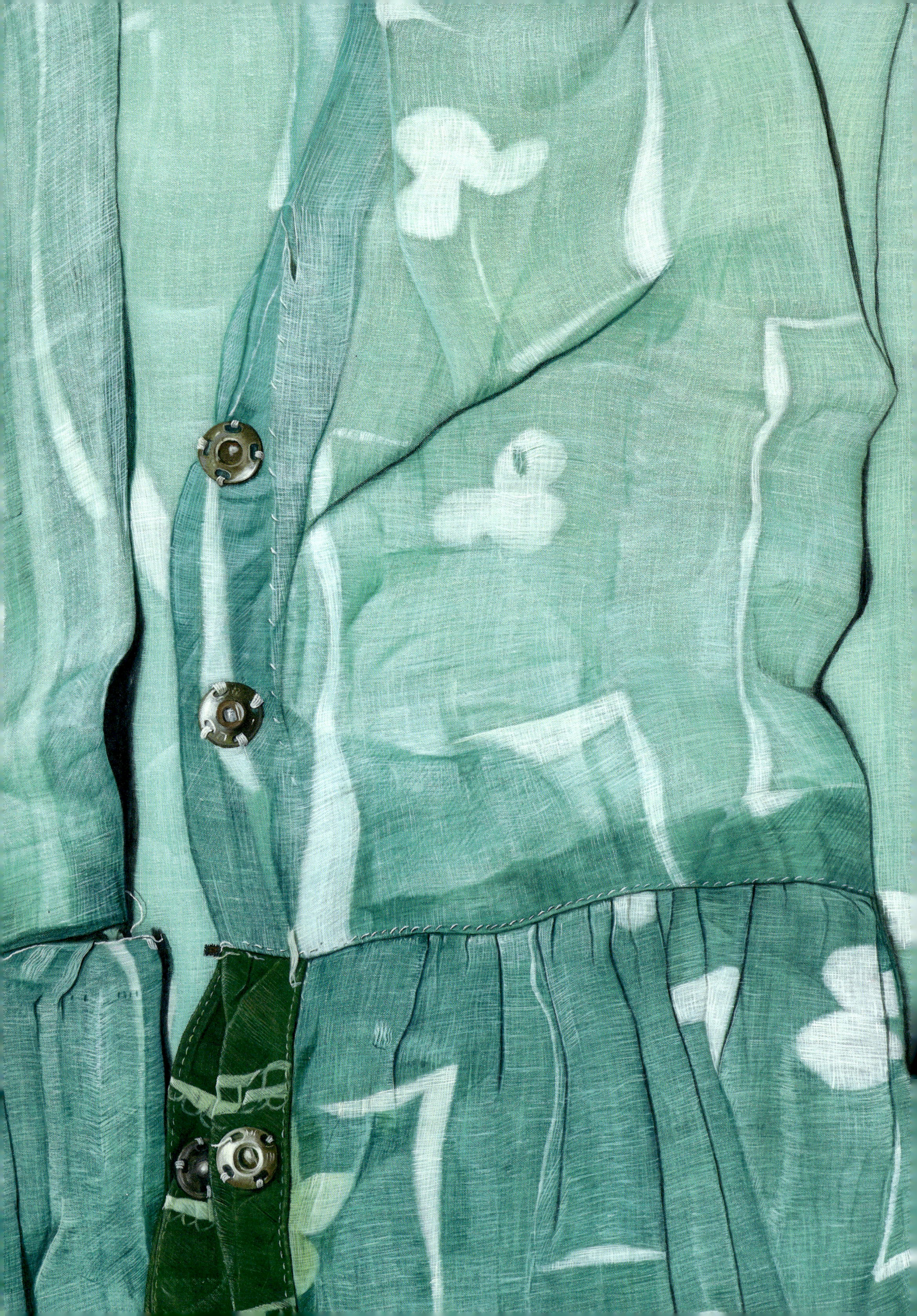

MARINA CRUZ
BREATHING PATTERNS

With a text by Kira Jürjens and an interview with the artist by Philipp Bollmann

DISTANZ

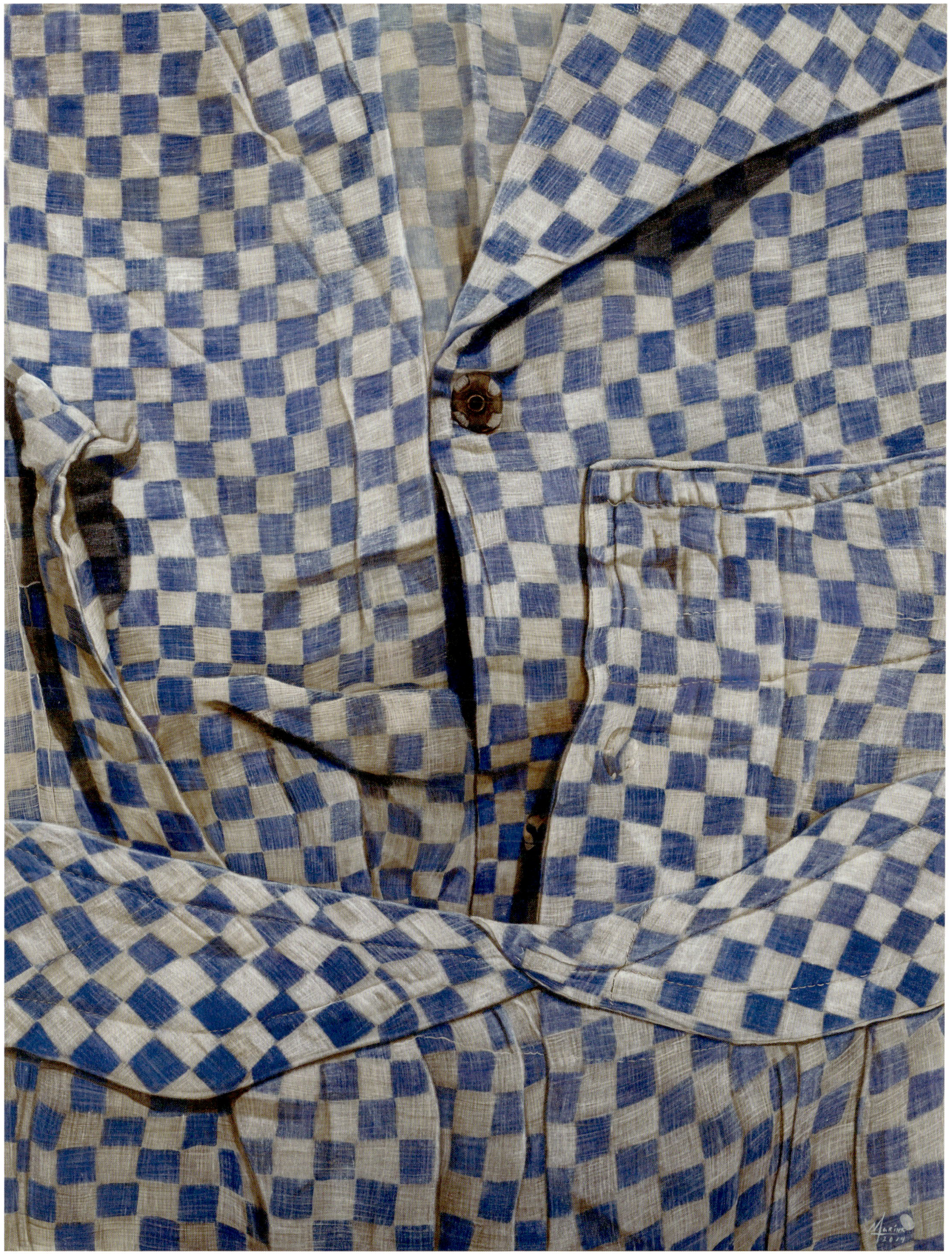

Chequered, 2014

White Lines on Red Horizontals, 2015

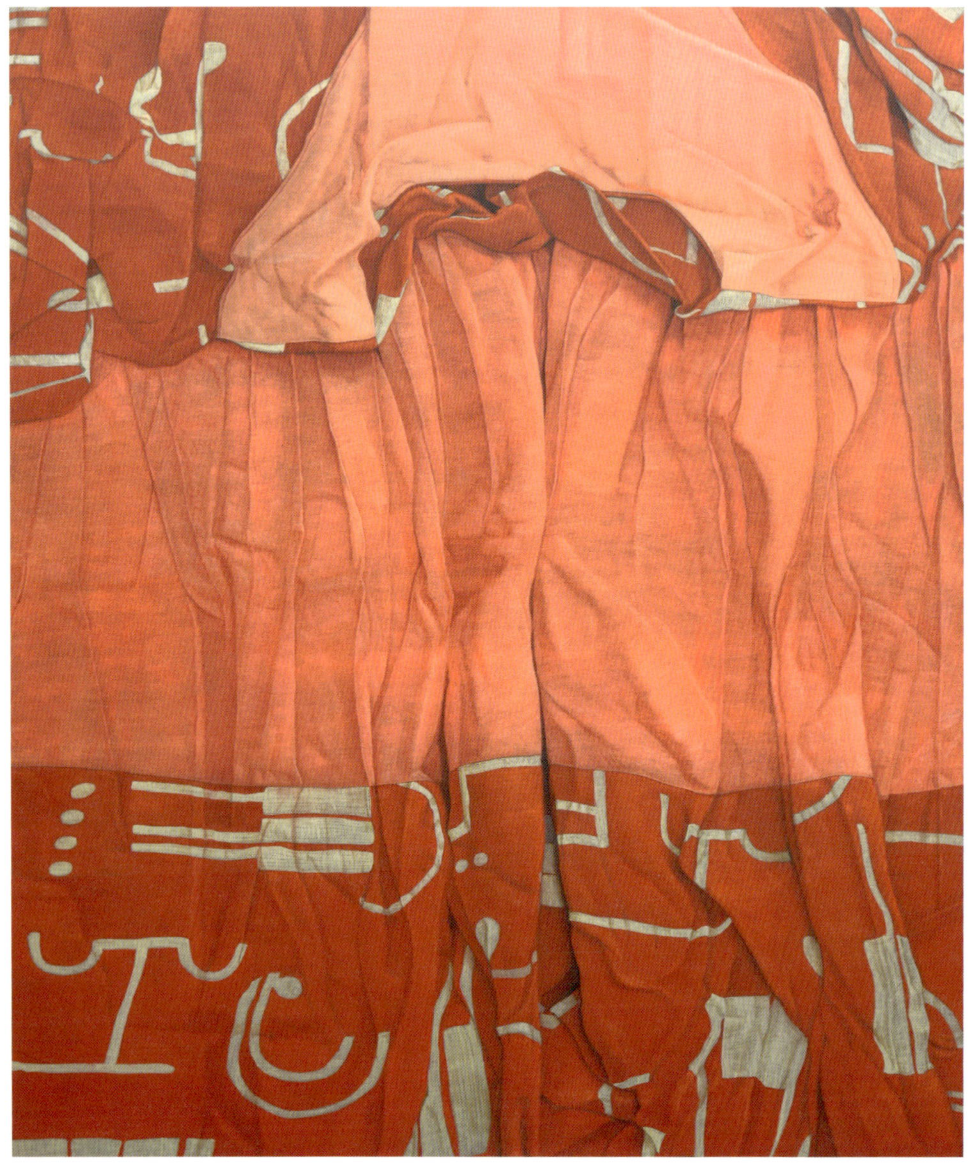

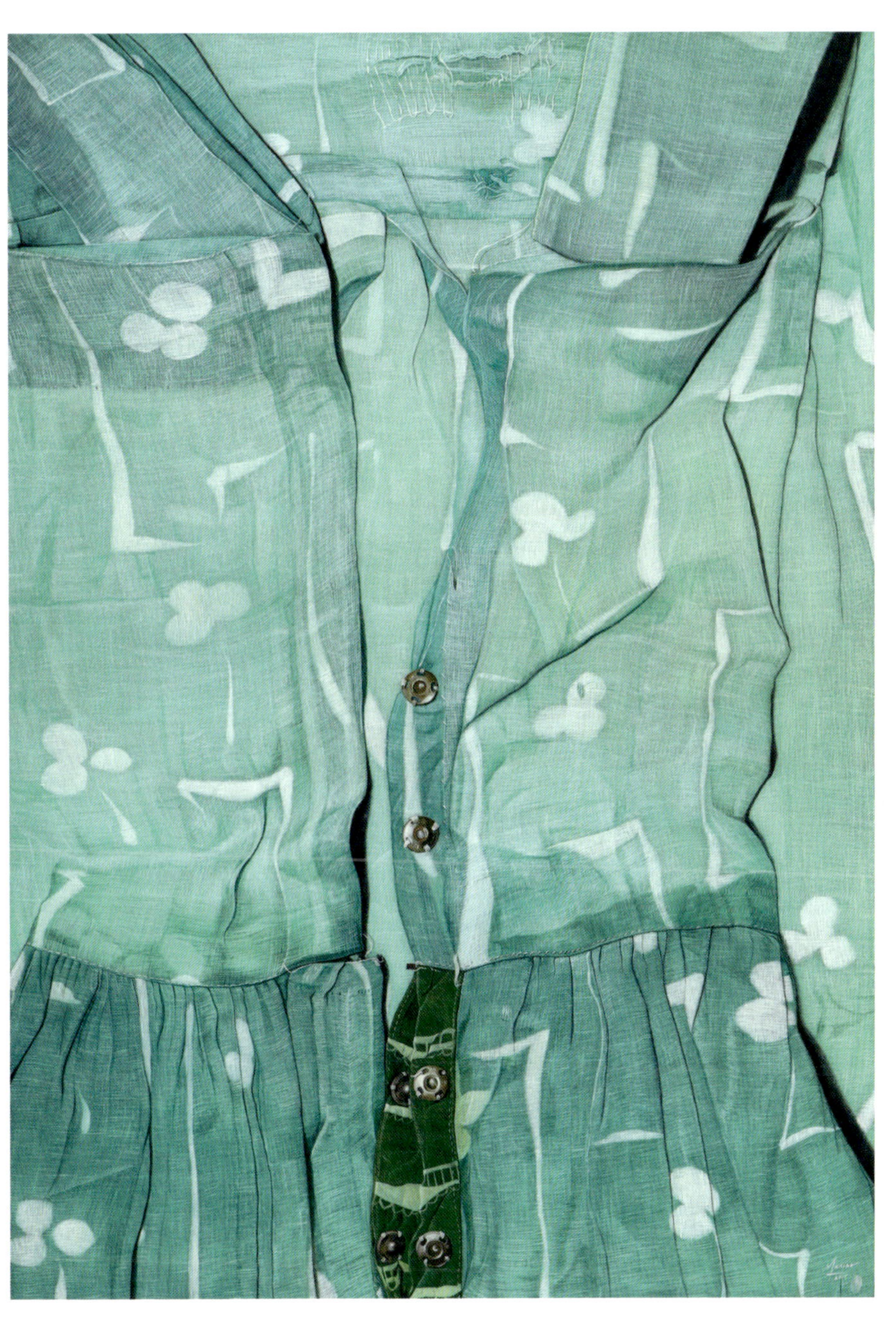

Faded Green and White Clover, 2015

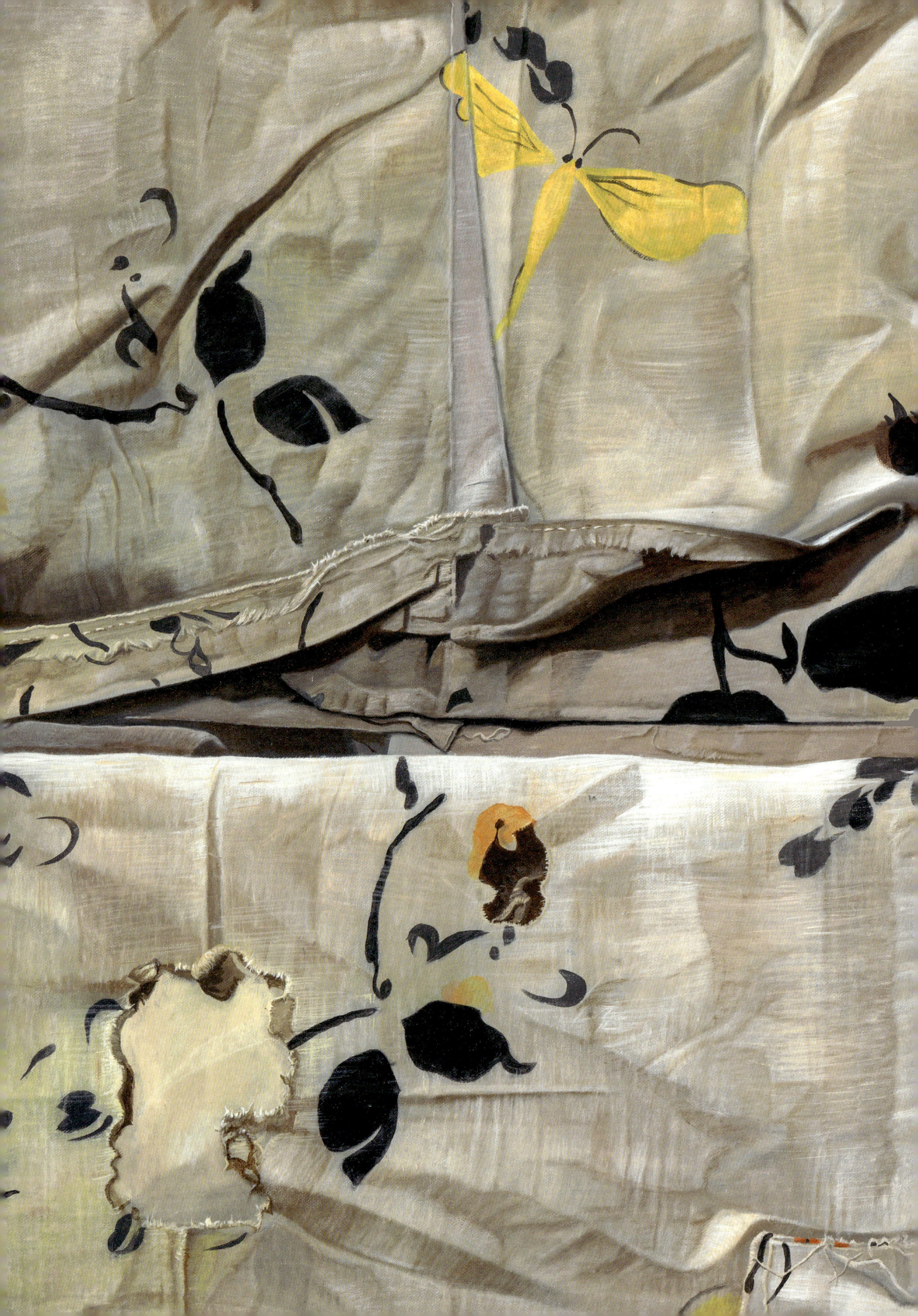

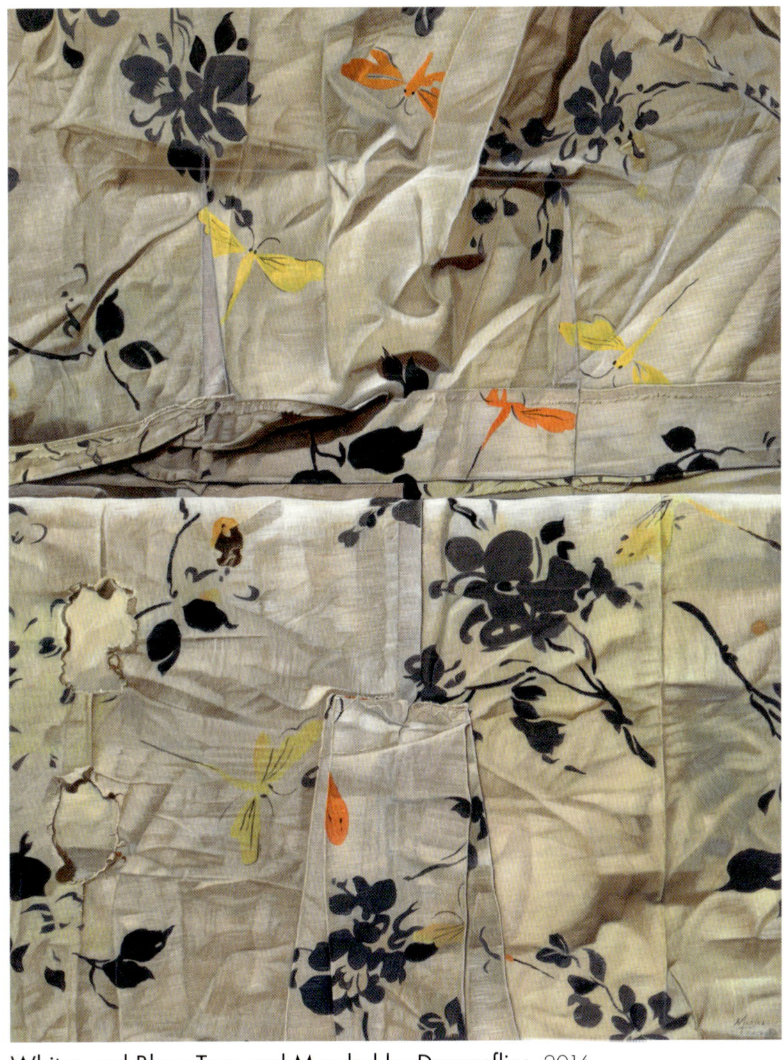

Whites and Blues Torn and Mended by Dragonflies, 2016

Stains and Shadows, 2014

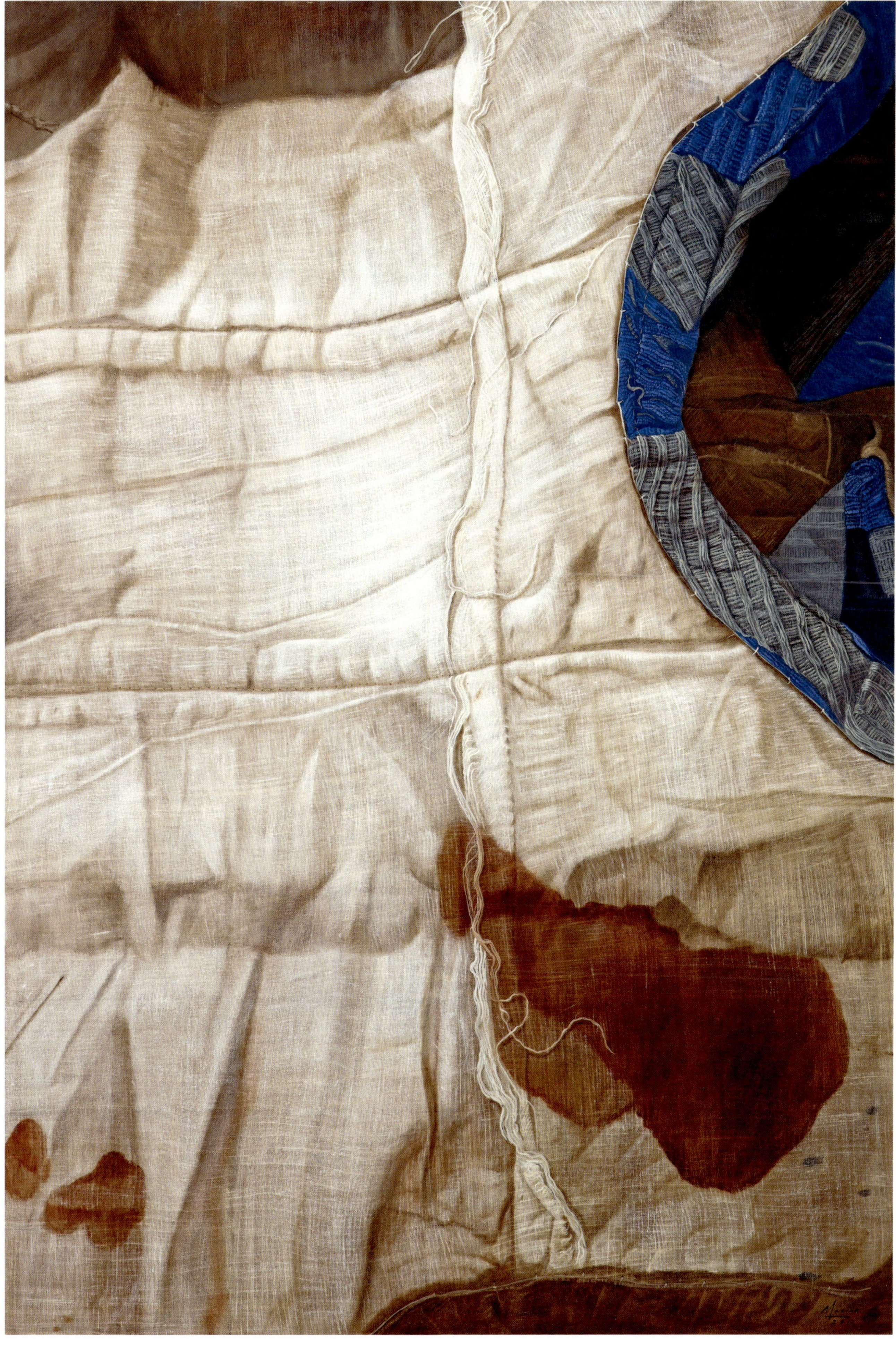

Red and White Stripes, 2014

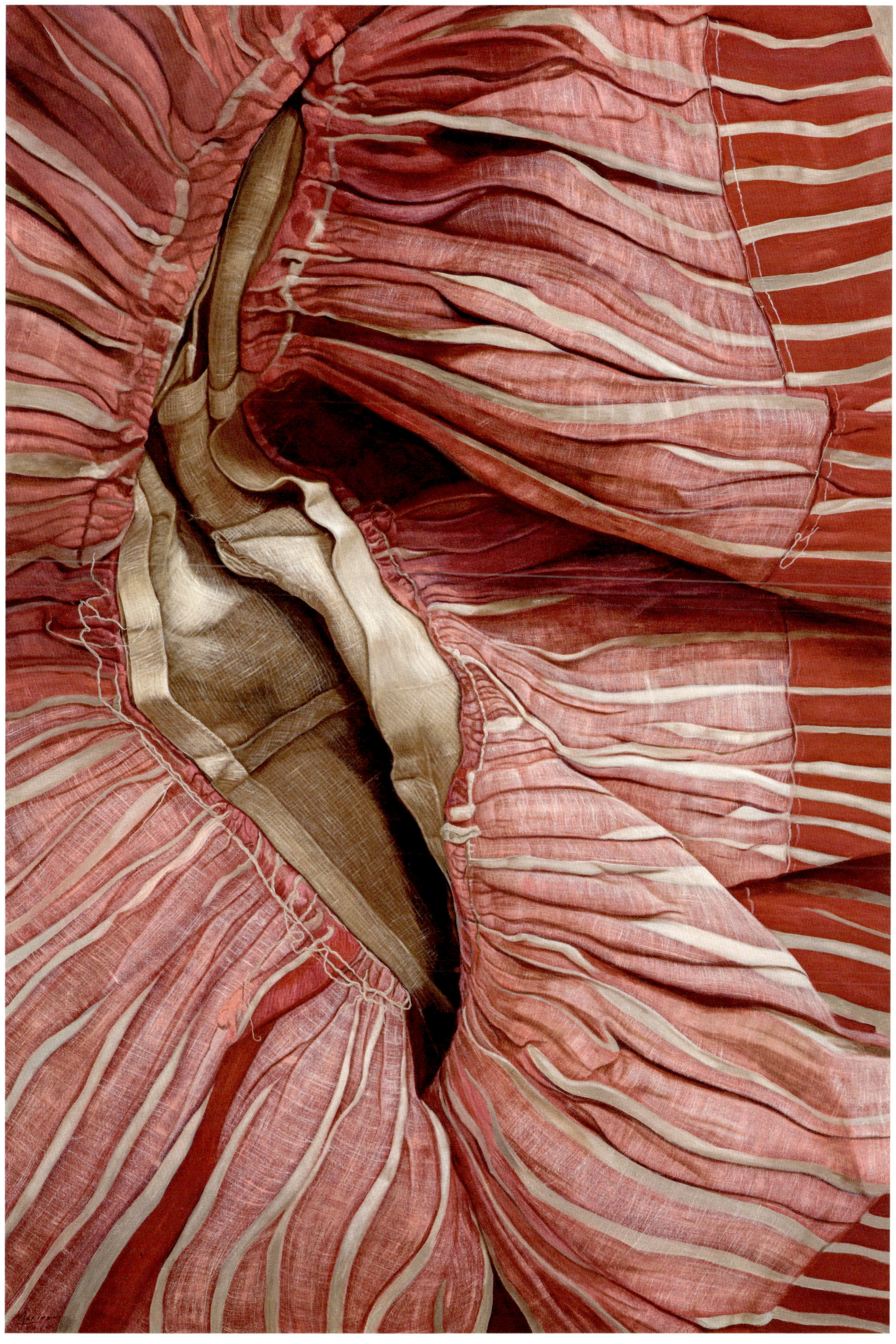

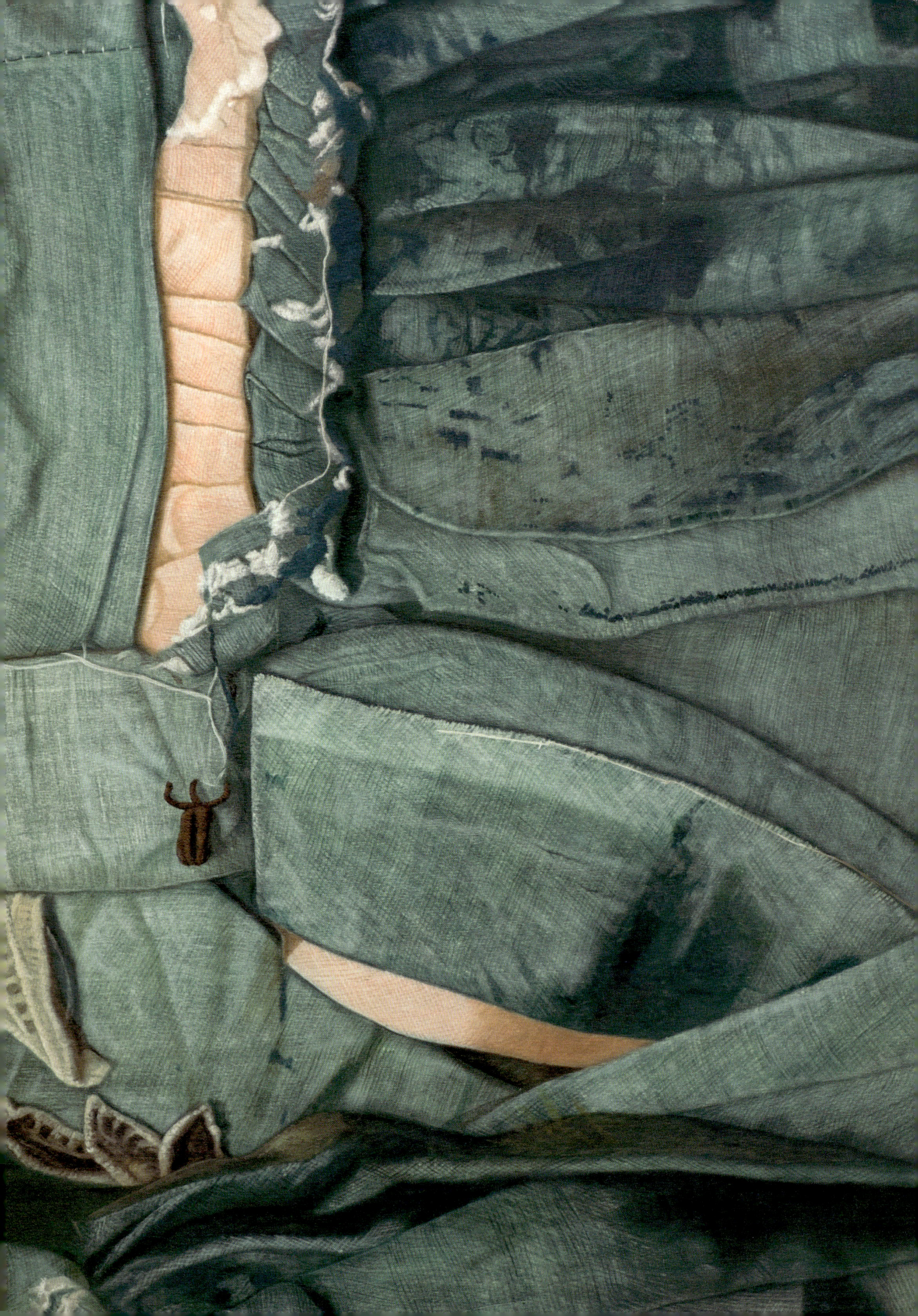

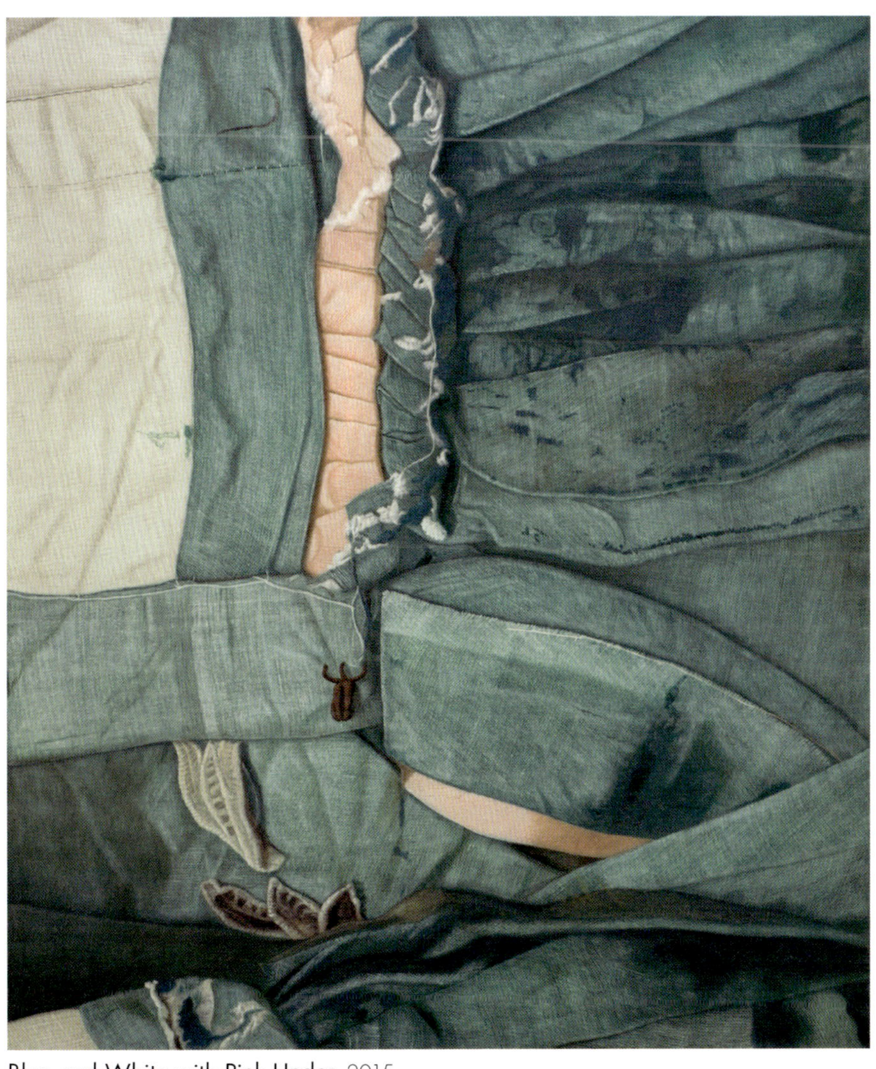

Blue and White with Pink Under, 2015

White Lines on Red Horizontals, 2015

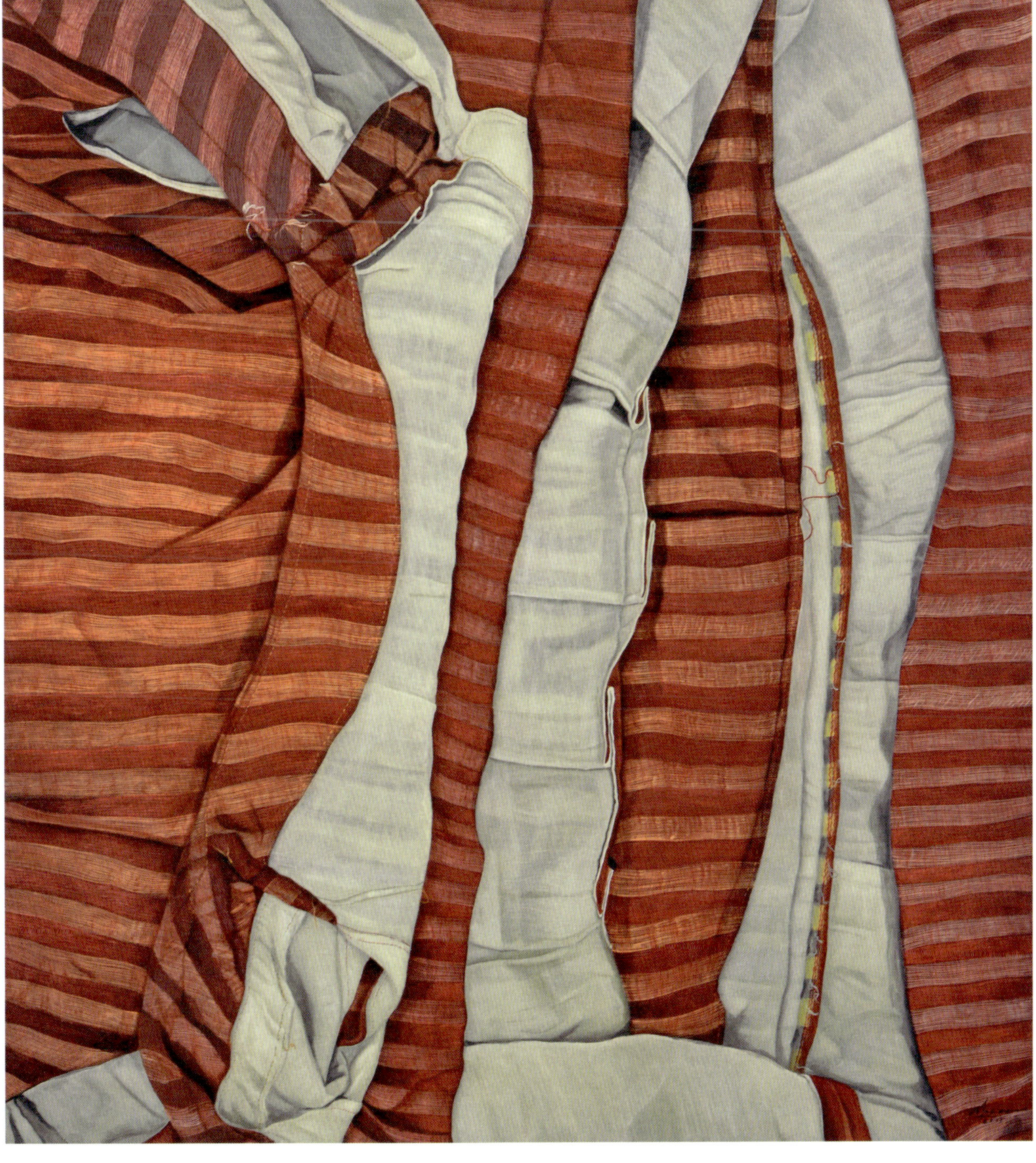

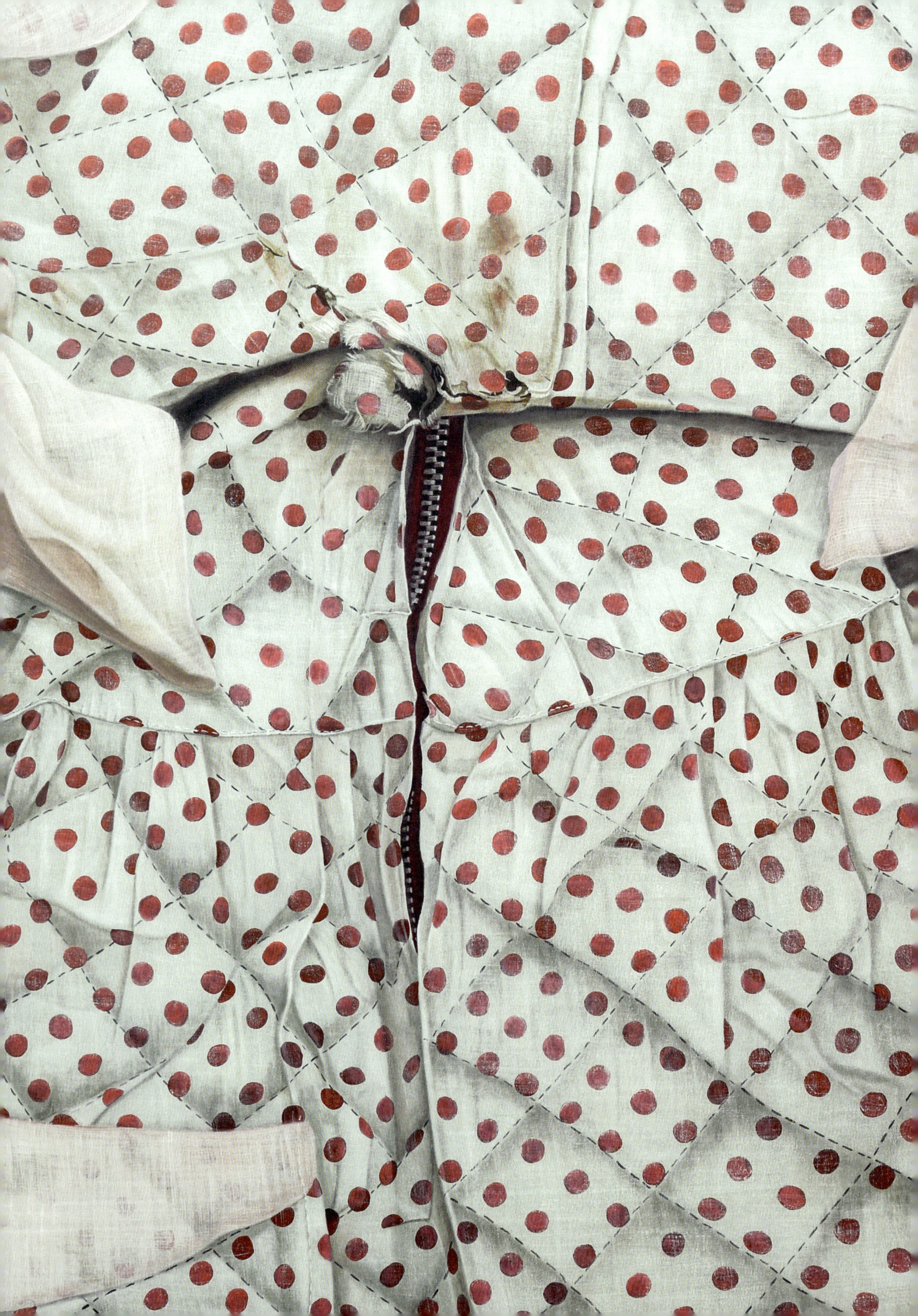

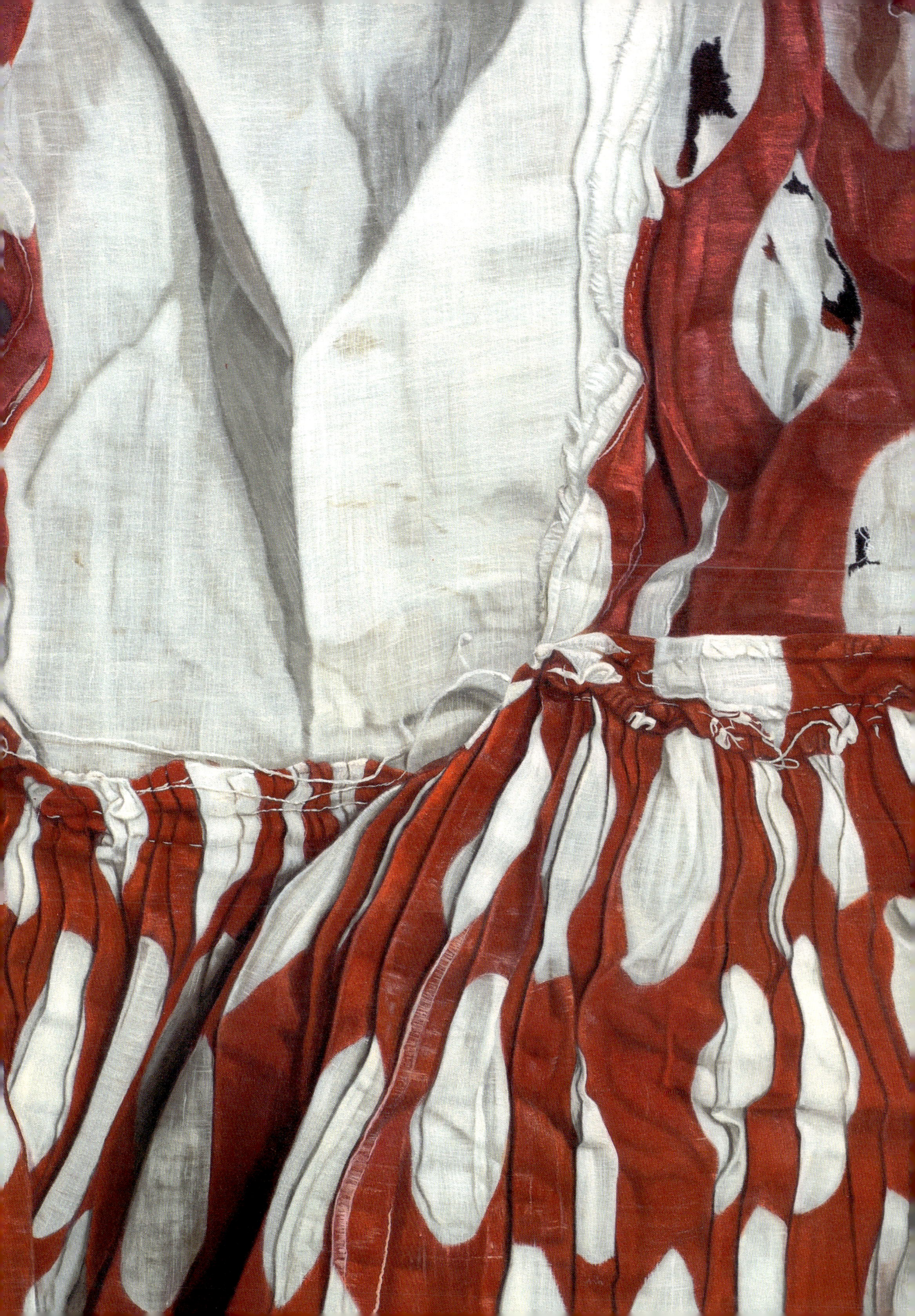

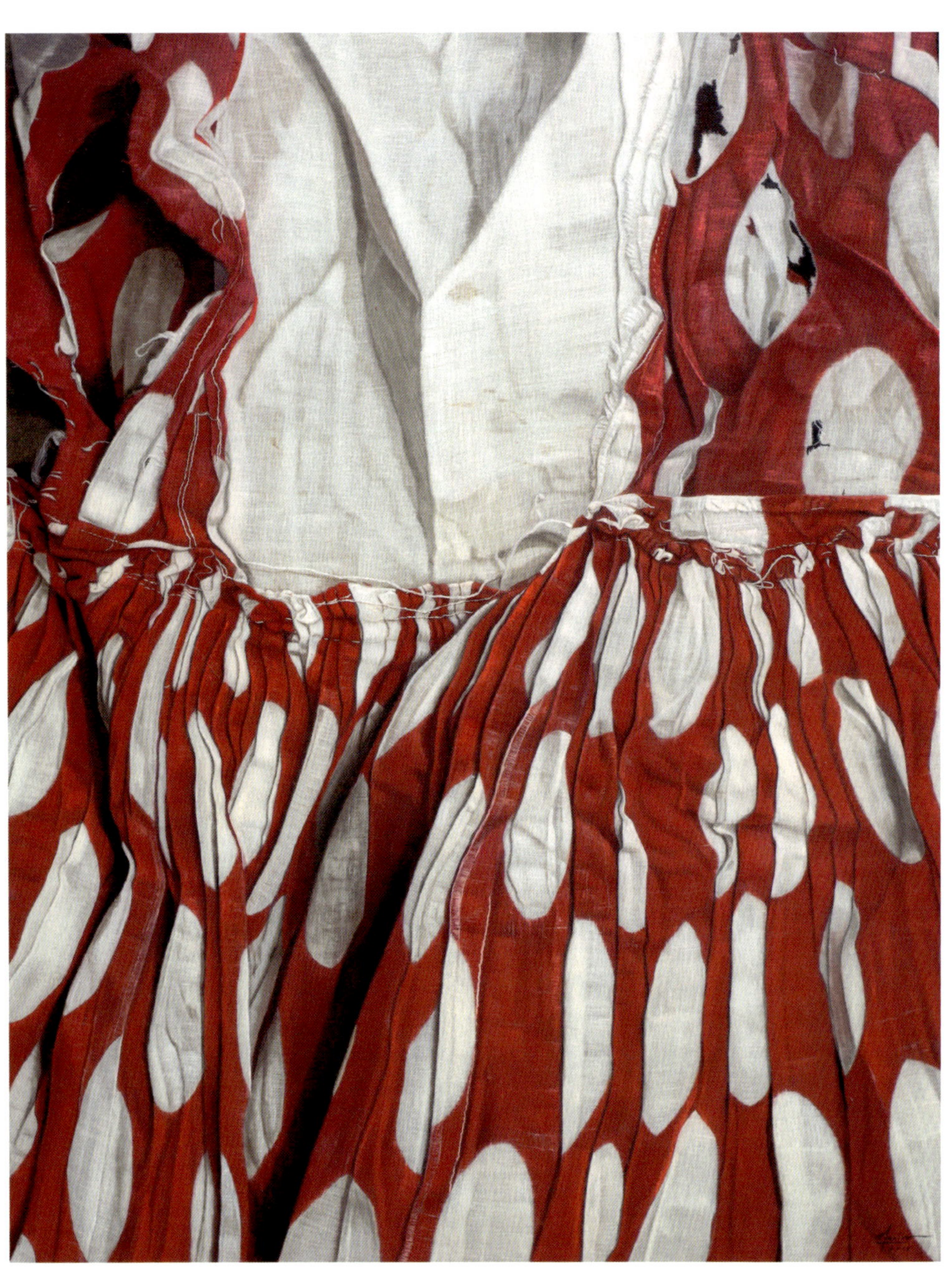

White on Red with Threads, 2015

Stains and Spots, 2015

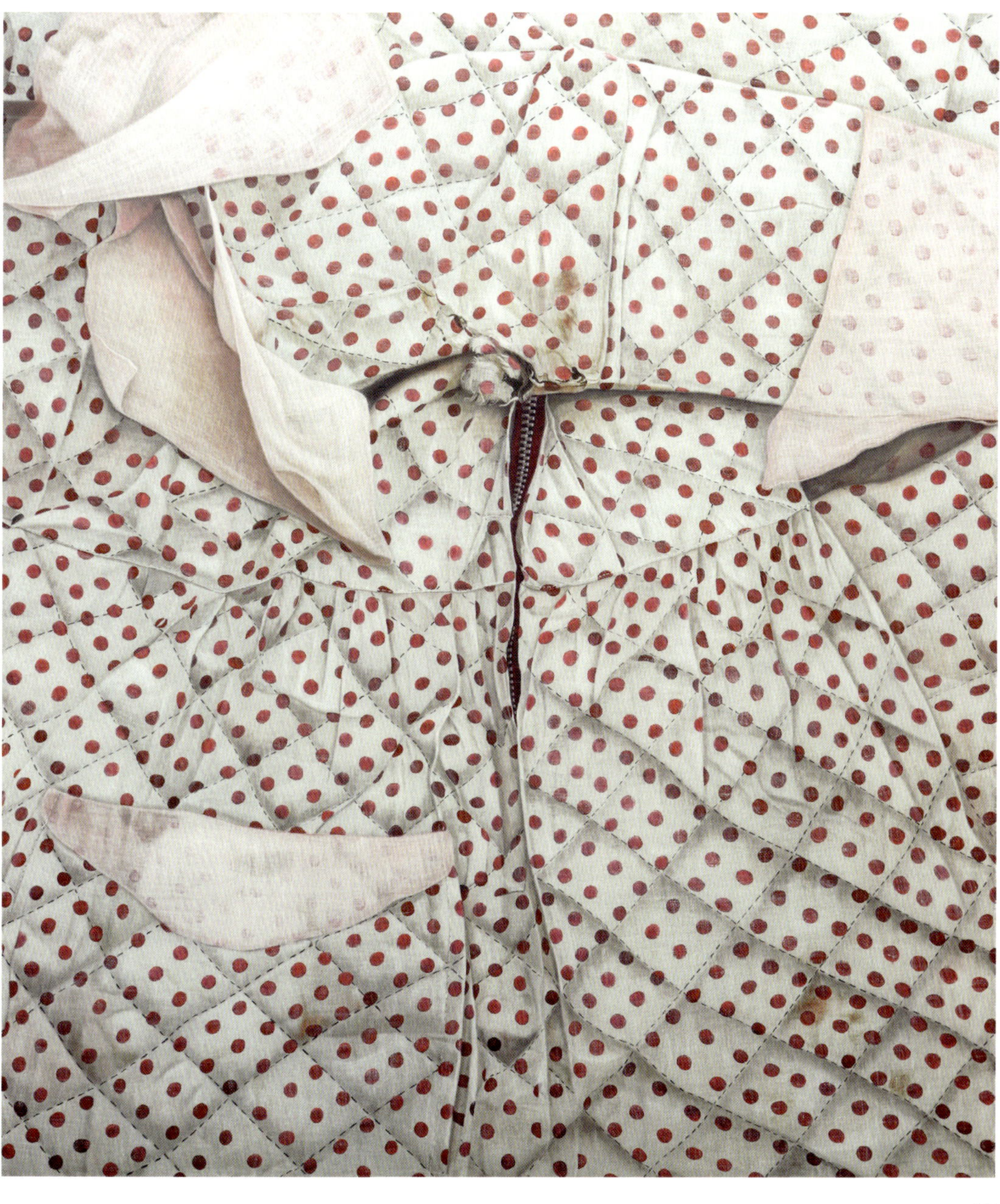

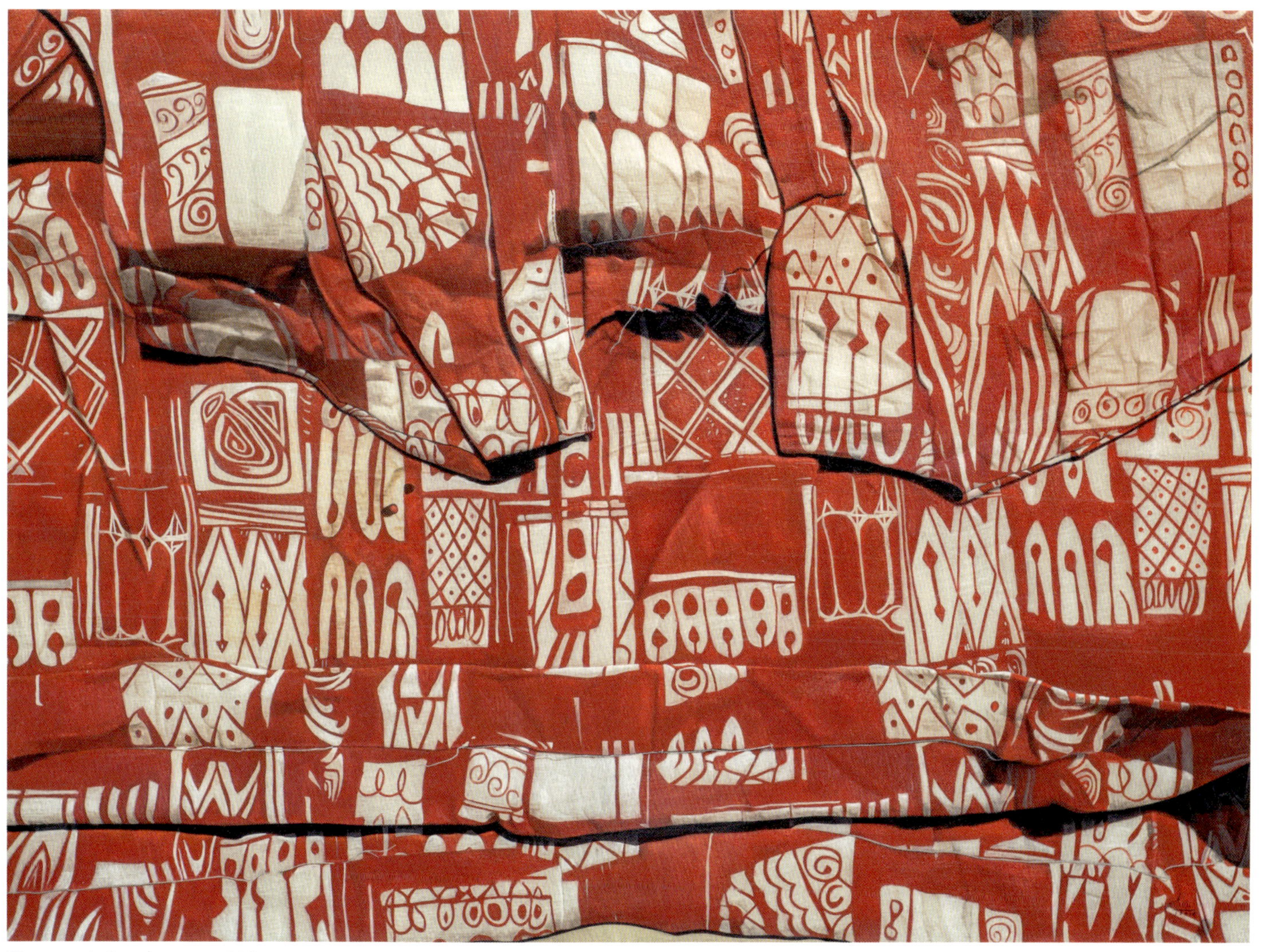

Geometric Landscapes, 2016

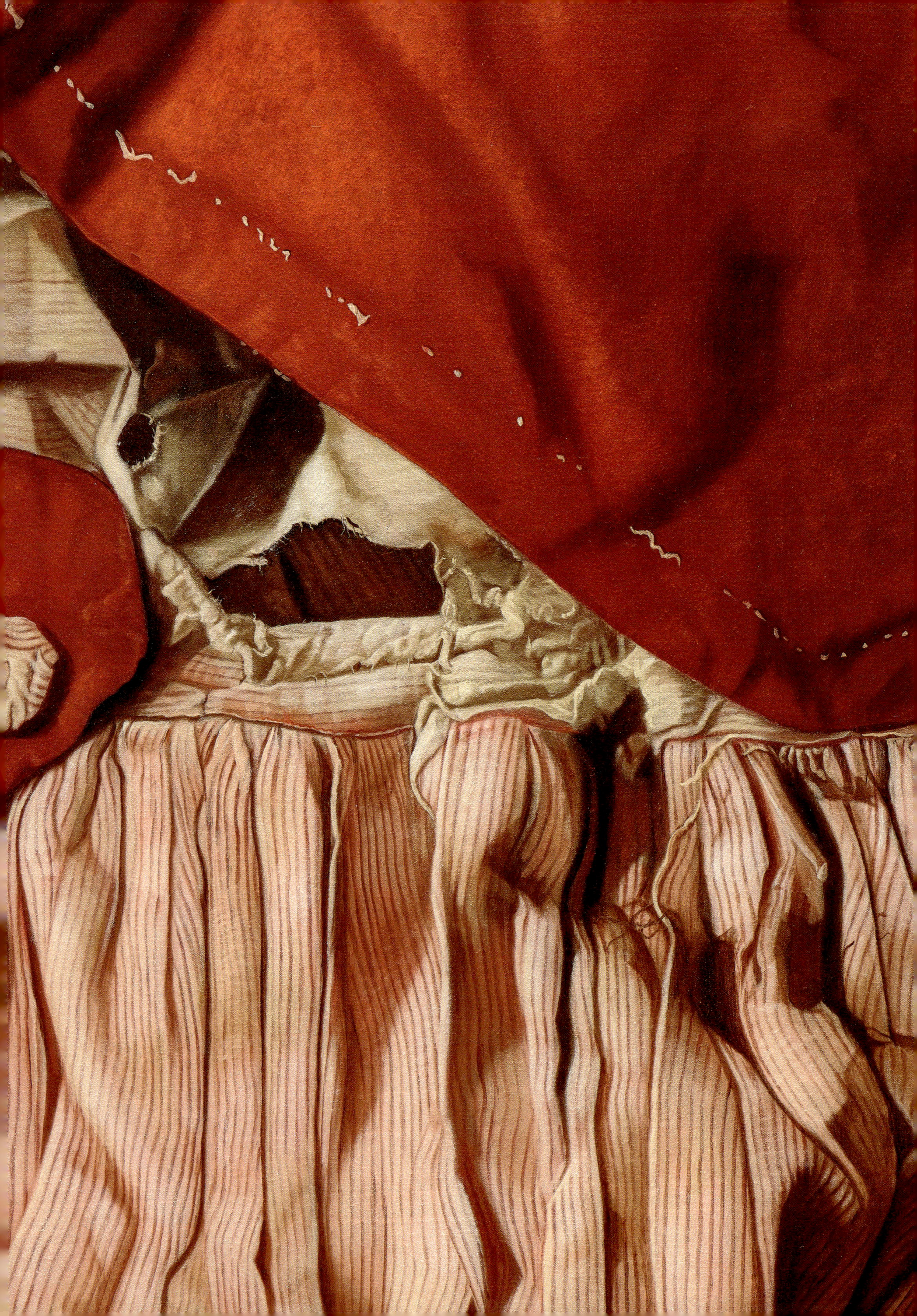

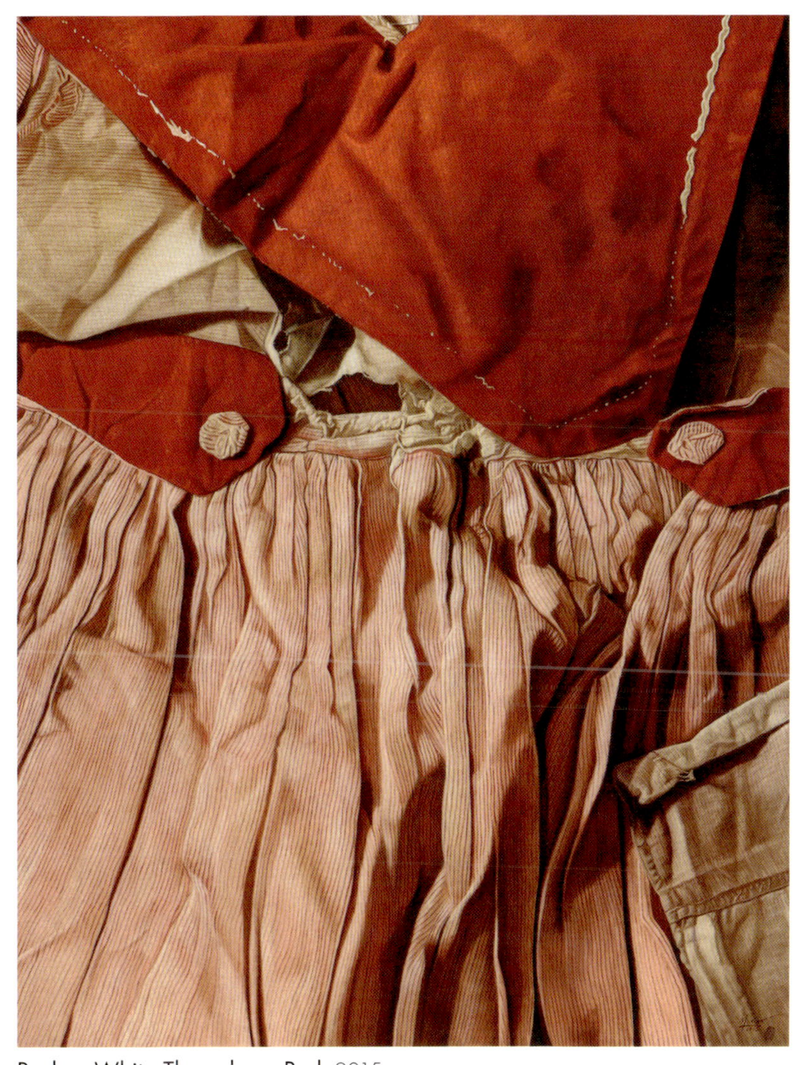
Broken White Threads on Red, 2015

Orange Flowers, 2015

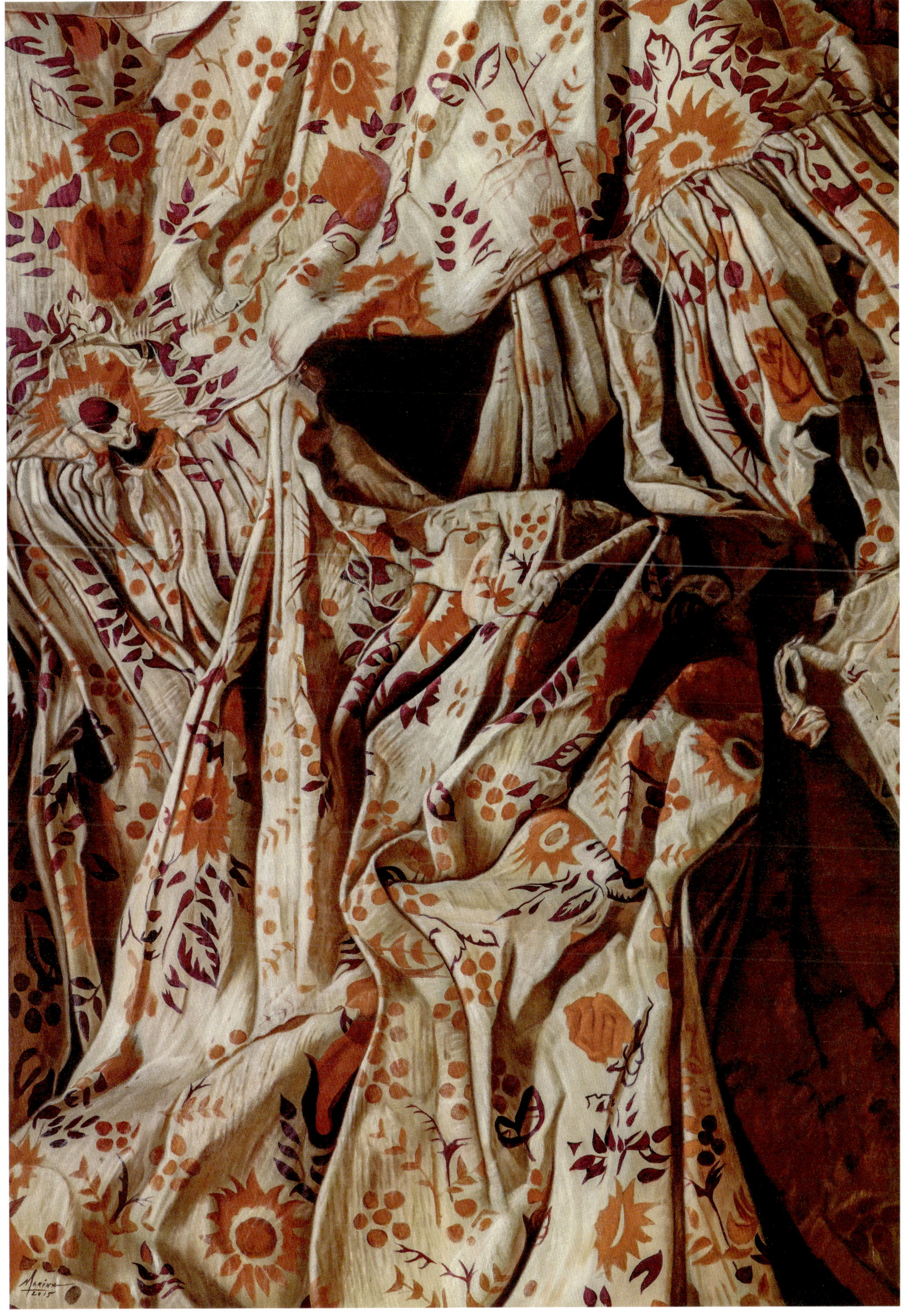

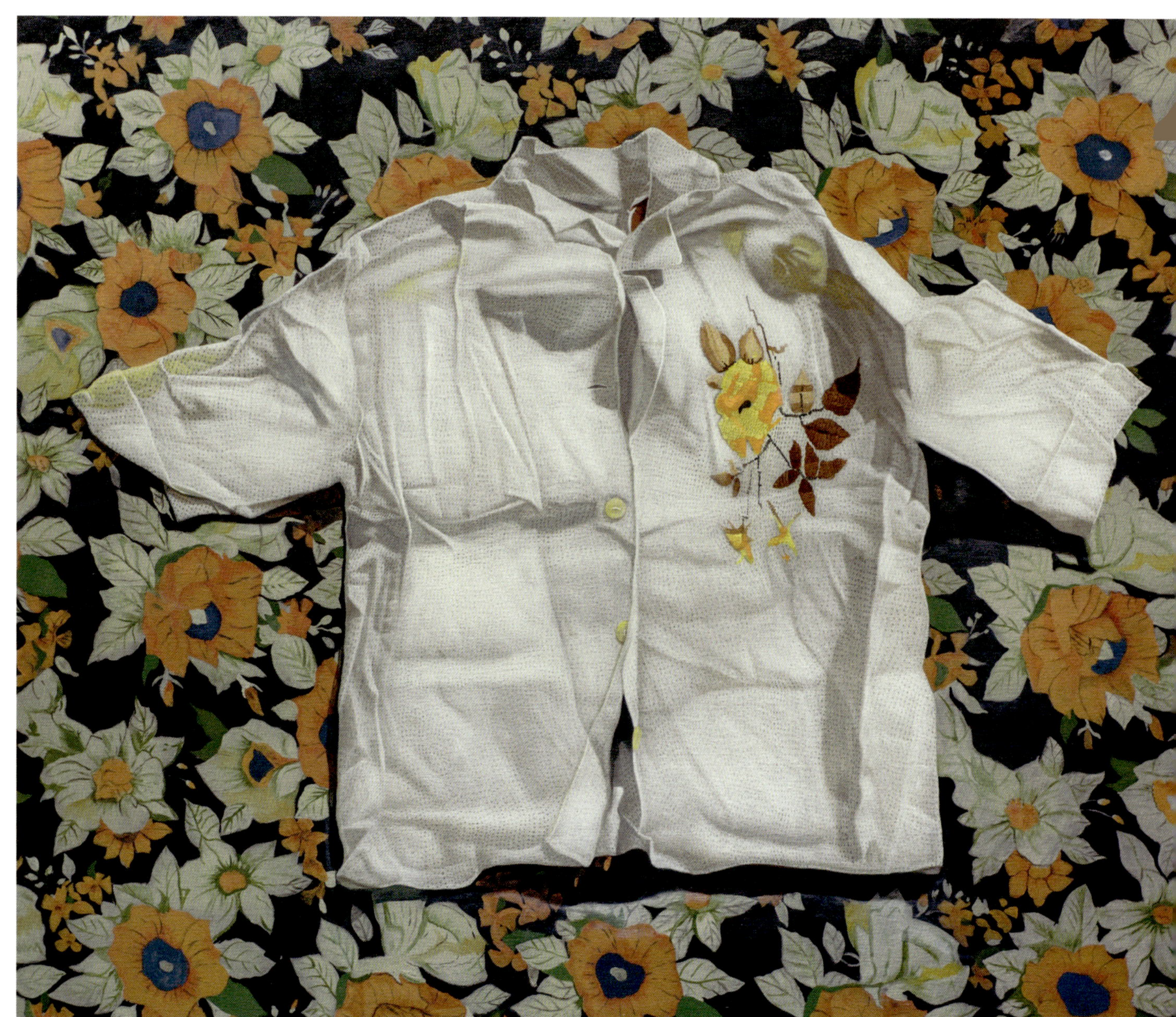

Edilberta's Embroidered Blossoms, 2015

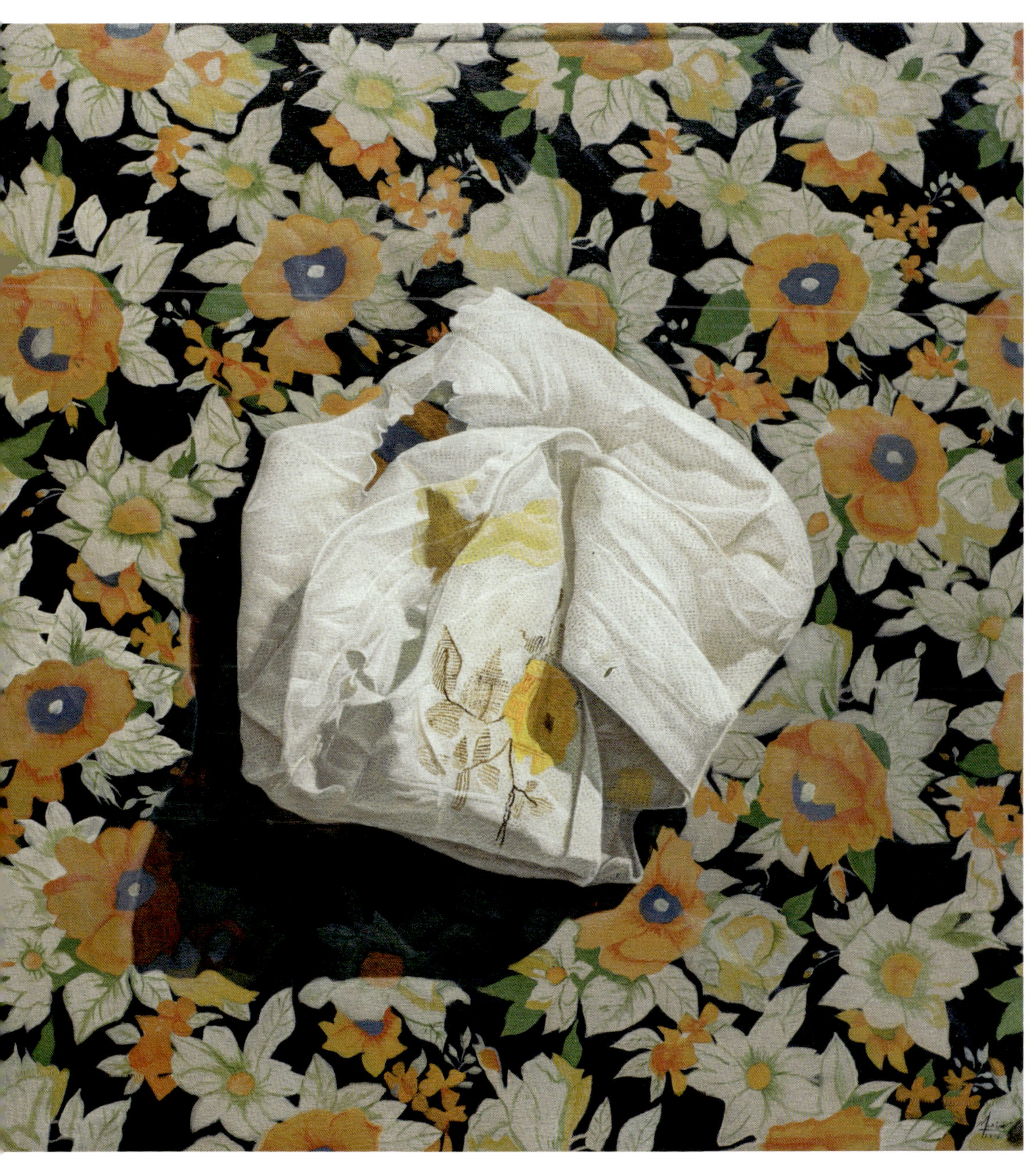

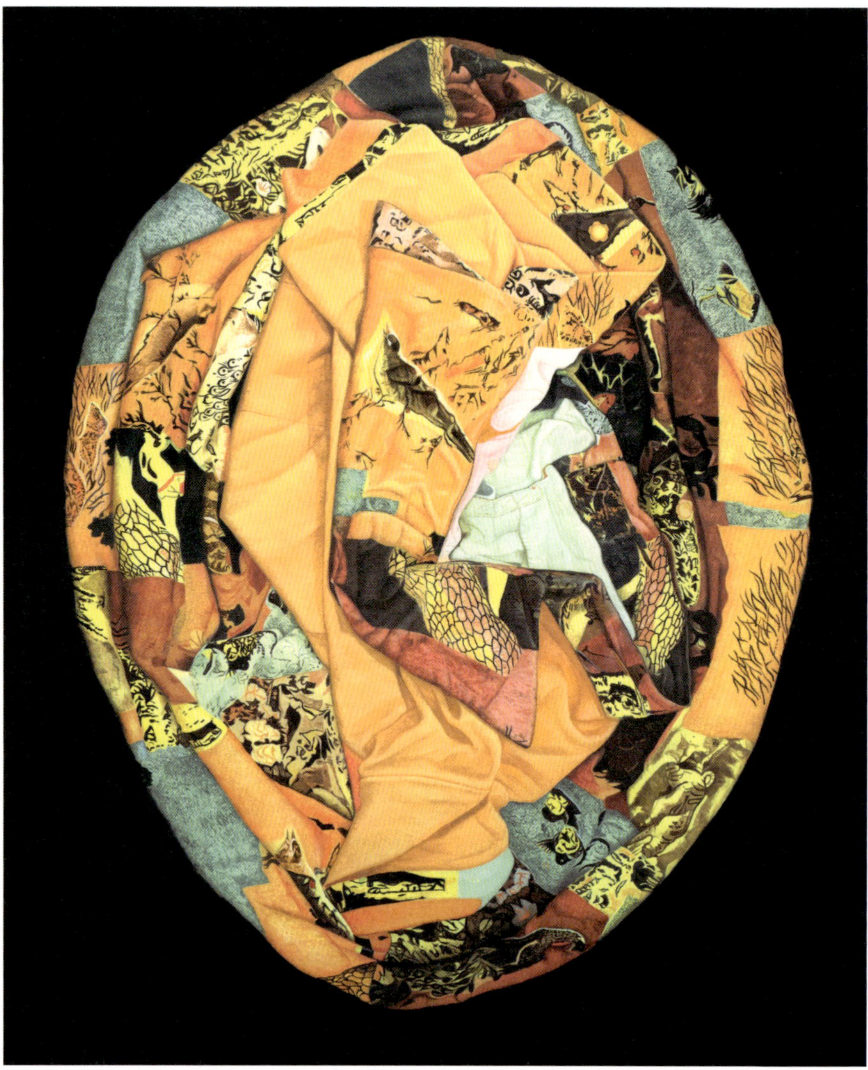

Nesting Patterns, 2017

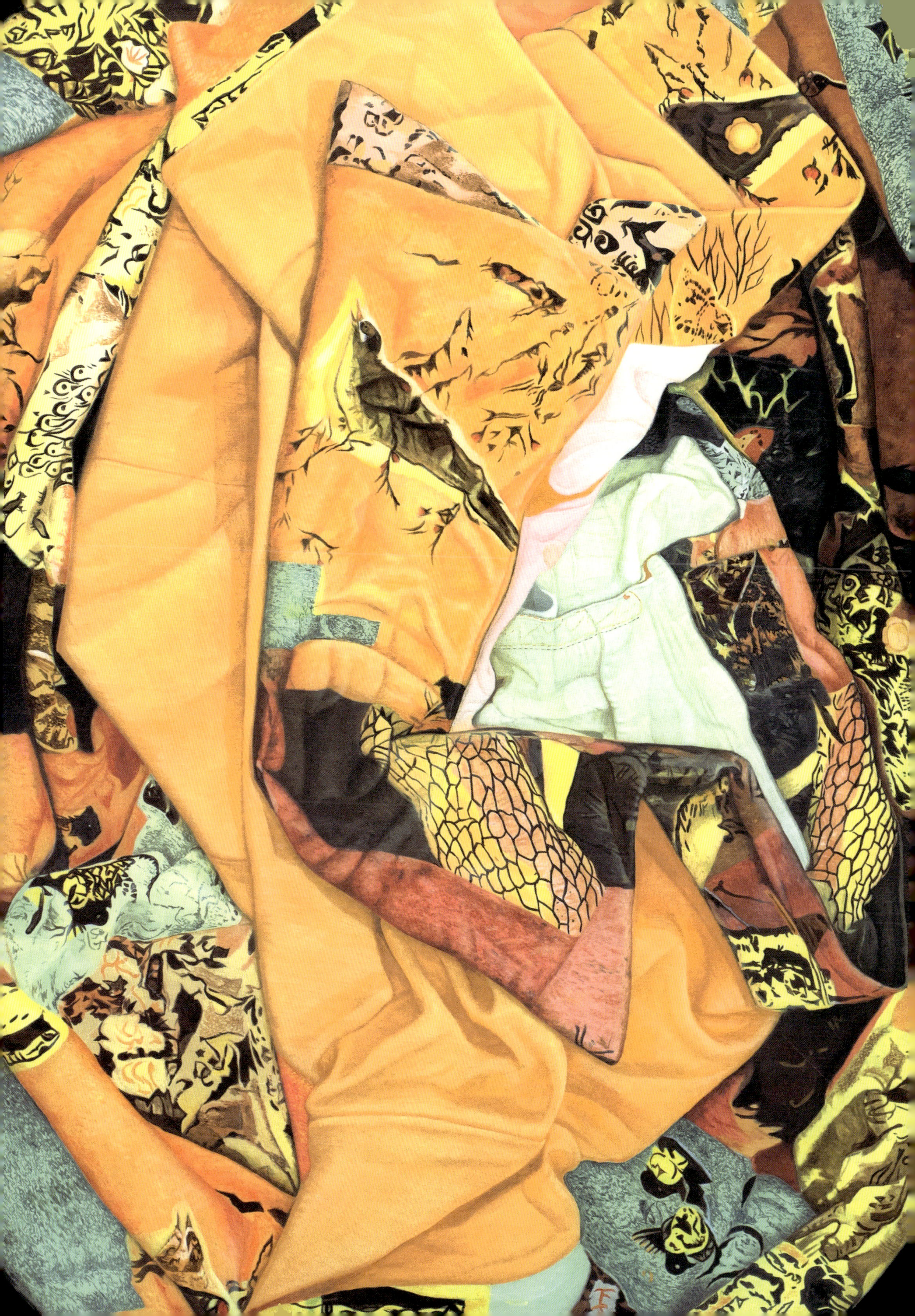

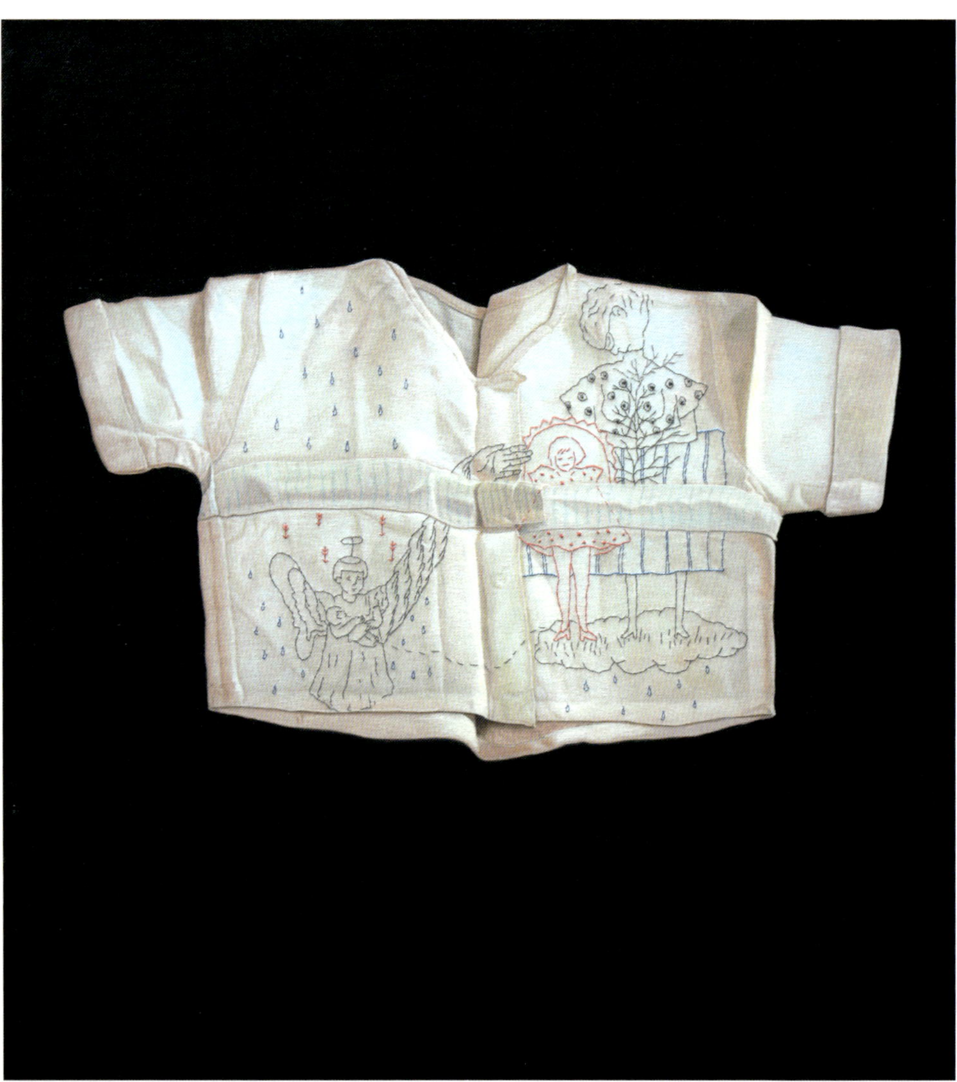

Security Blanket, 2015

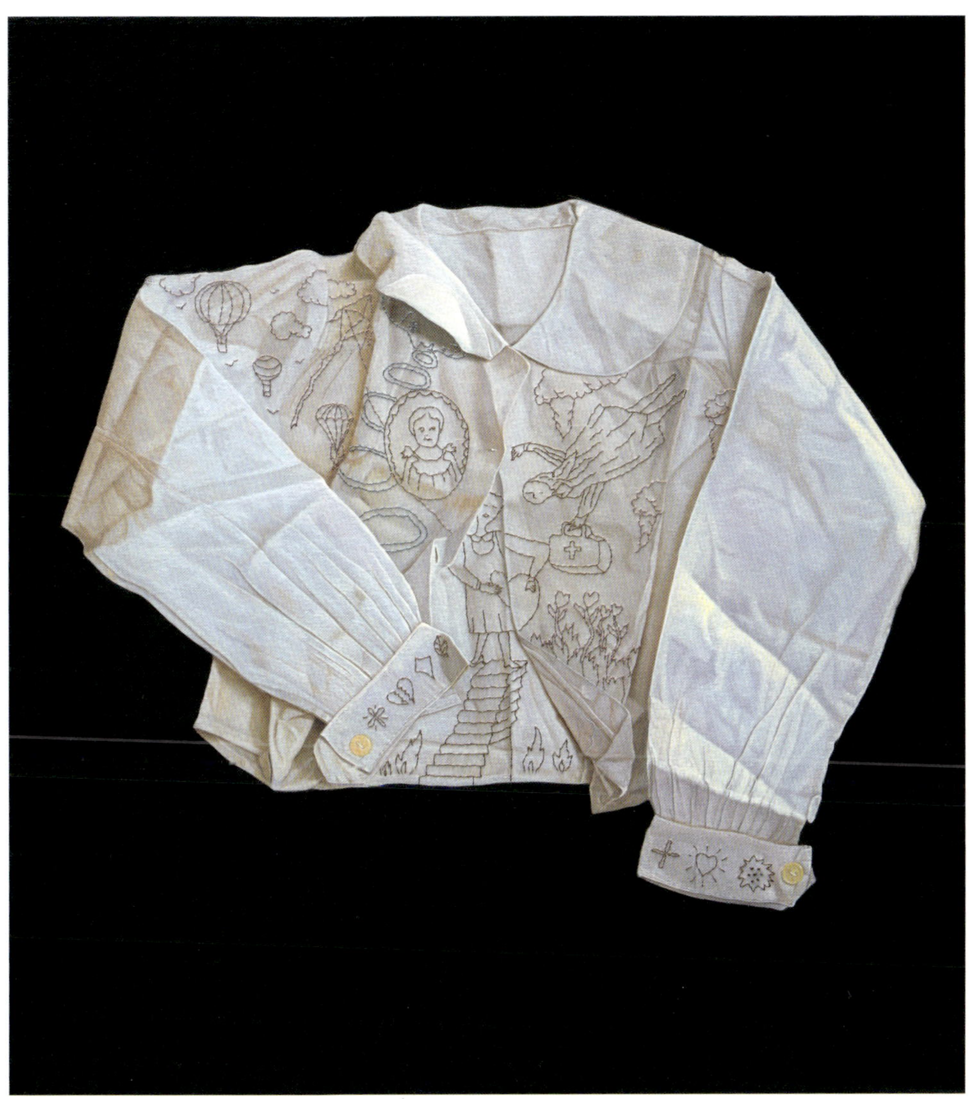

Flight and Plight, 2015

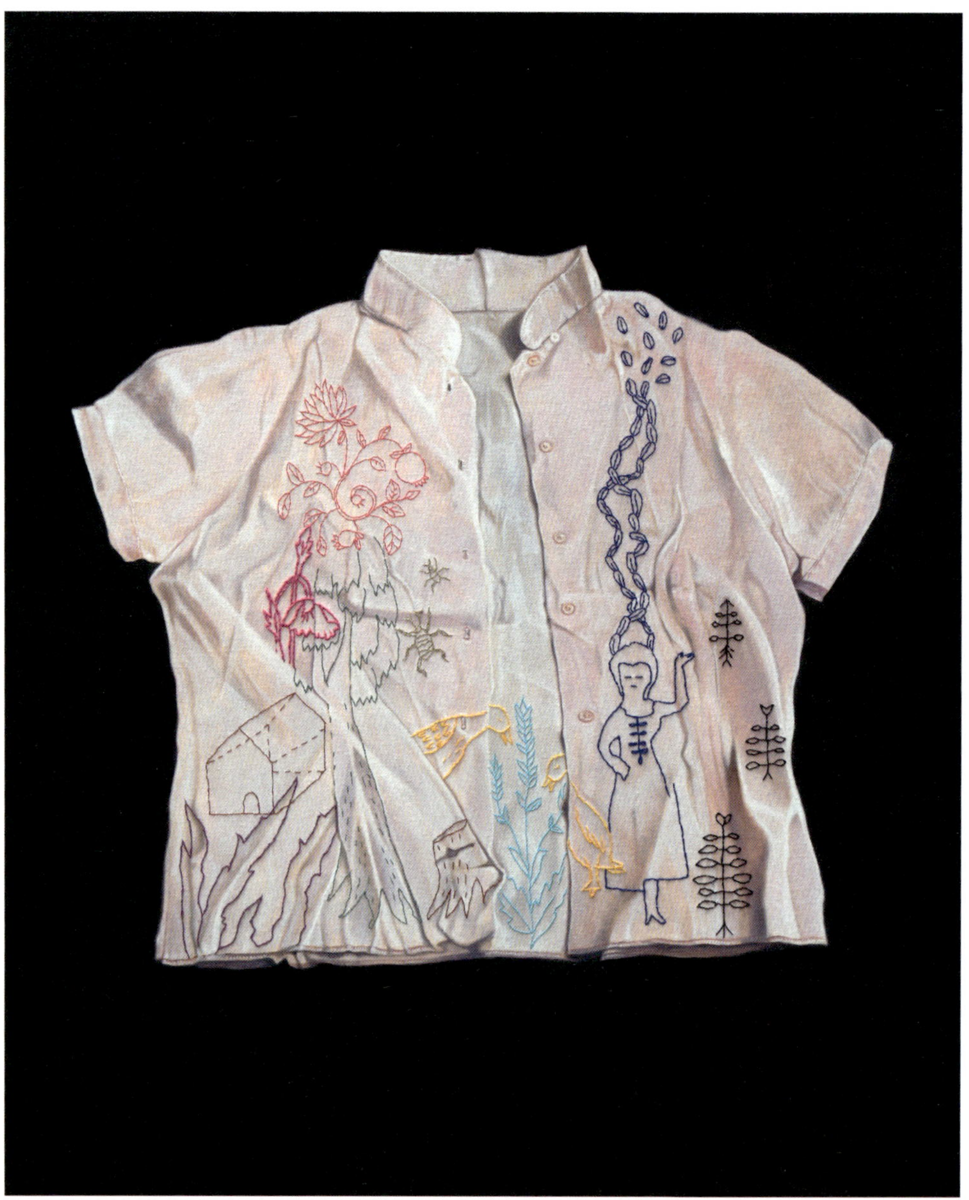

Lost Thoughts, 2015

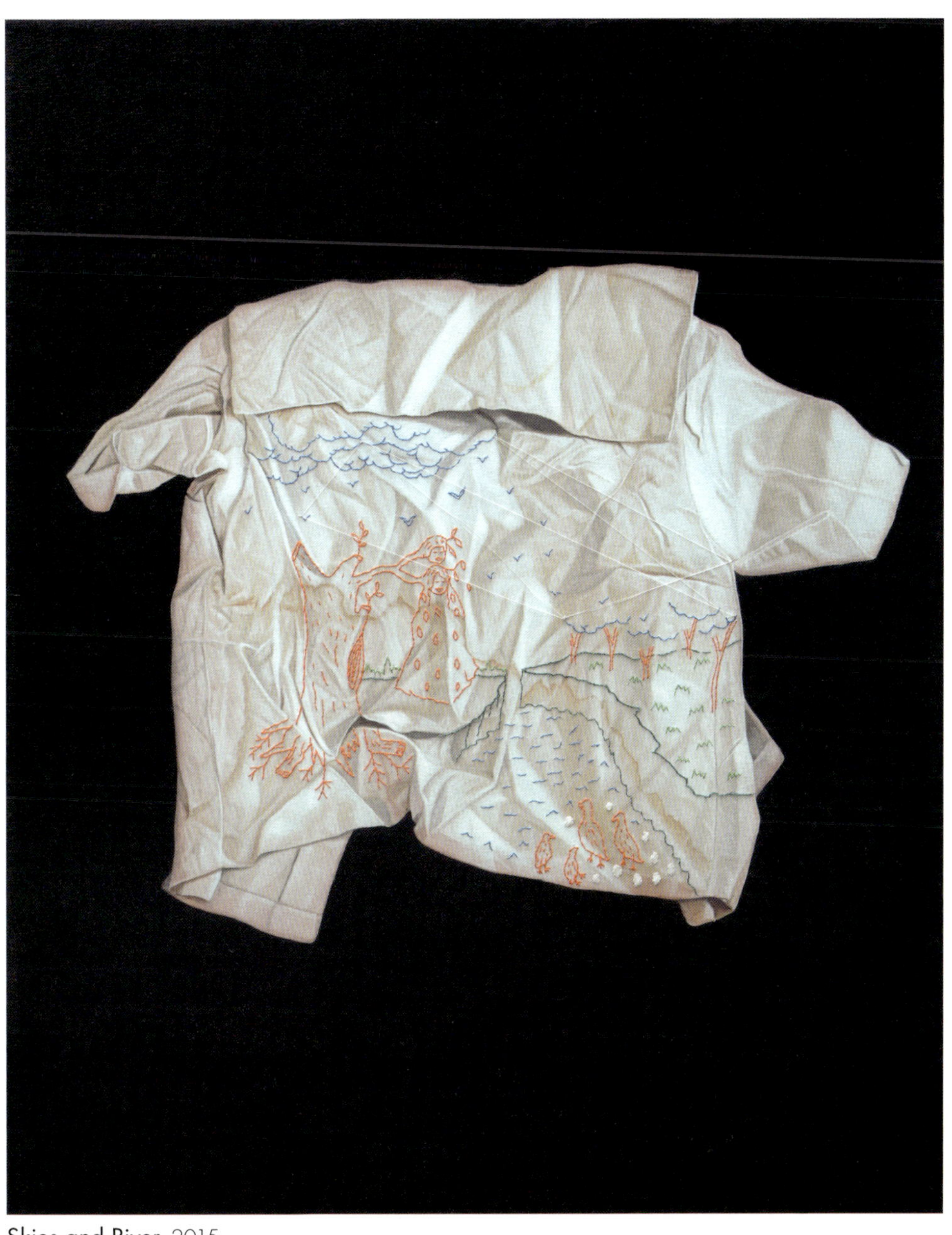

Skies and River, 2015

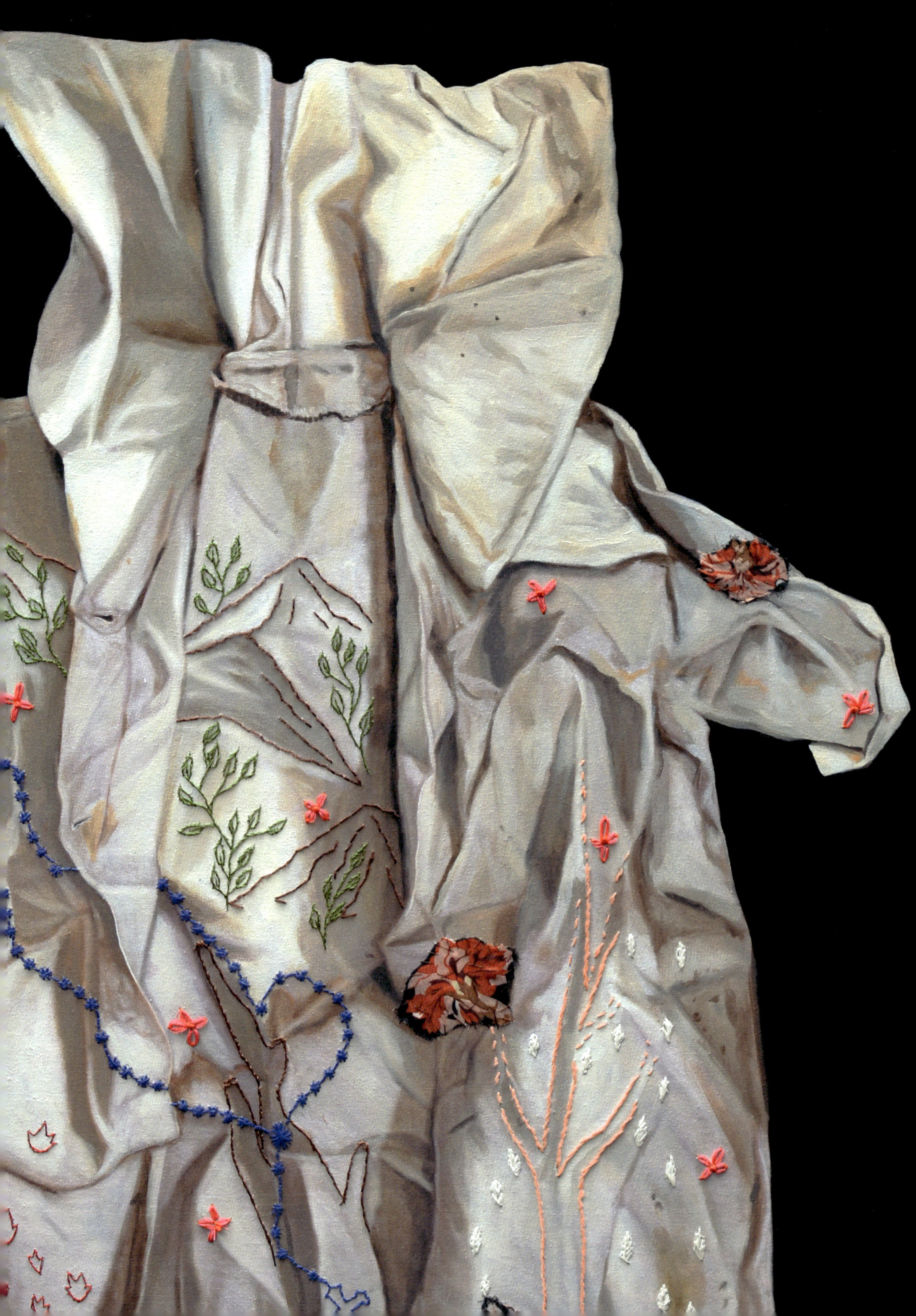

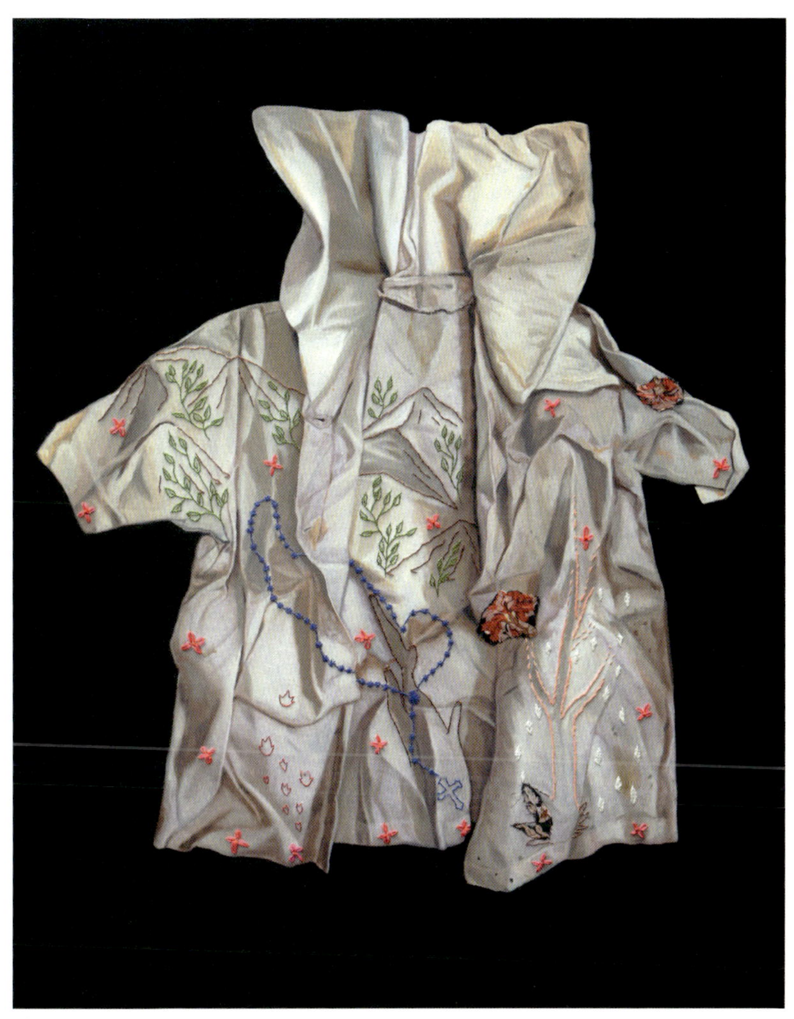

Mountainous Terrains, 2015

Flesh Underneath, 2017

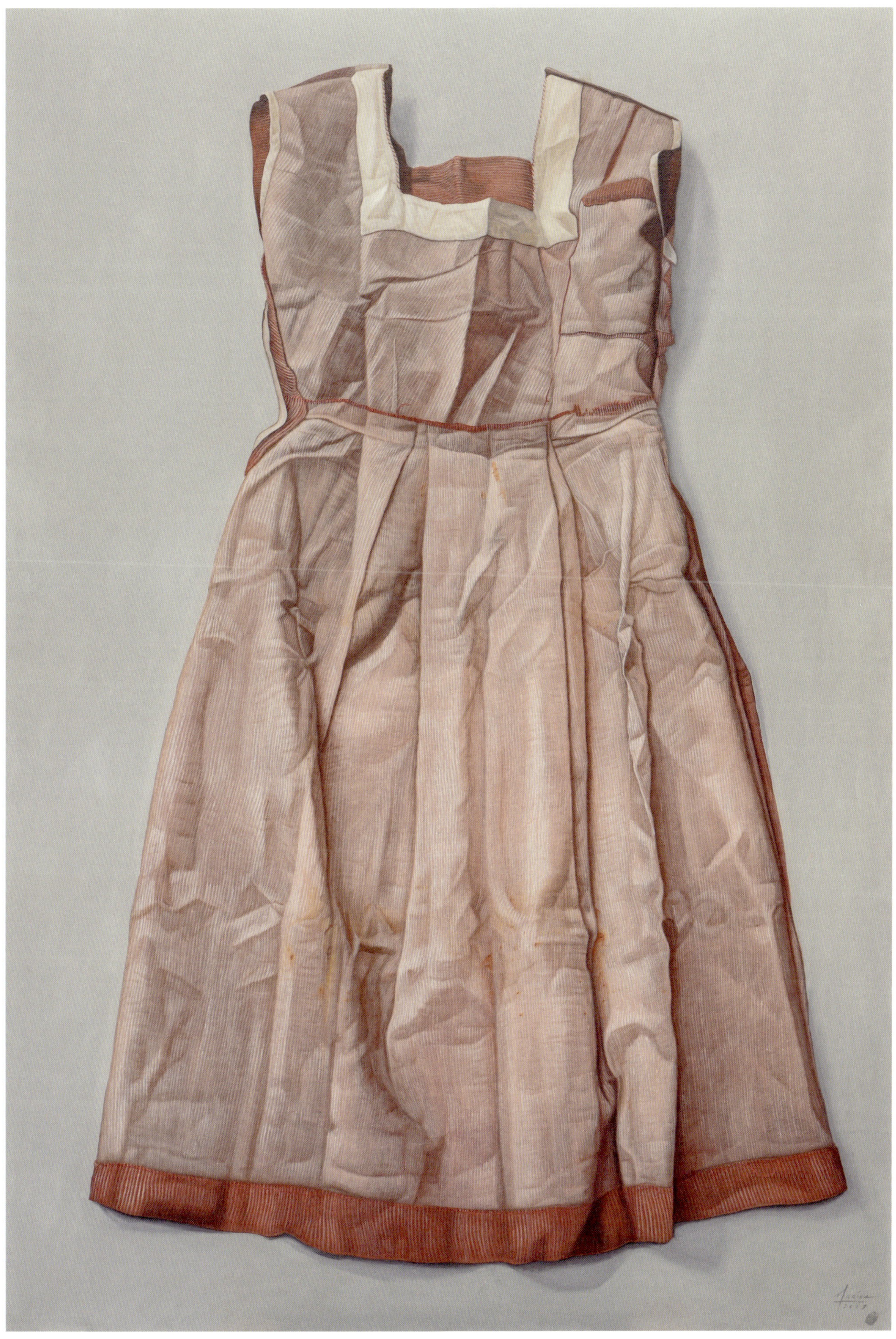

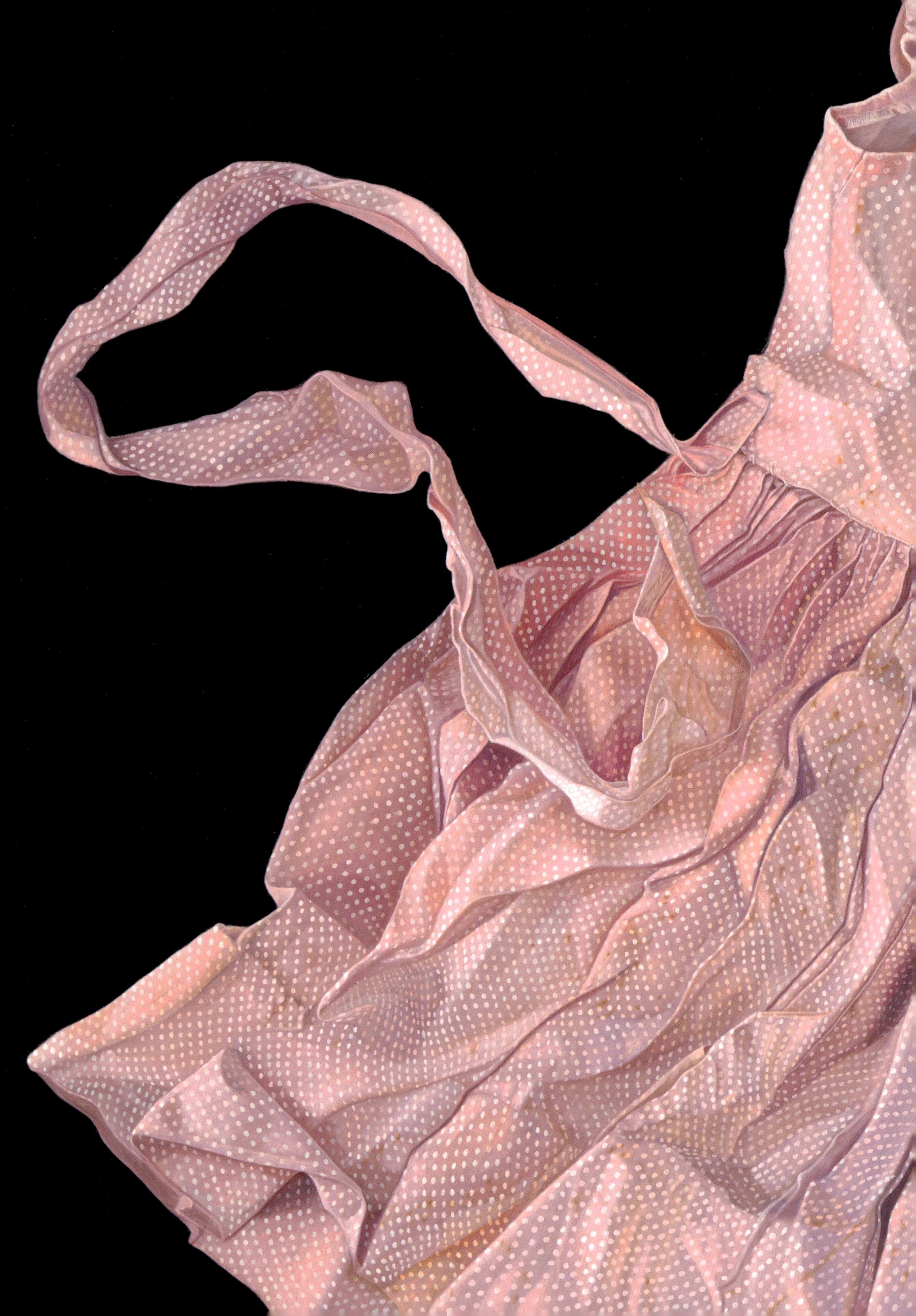

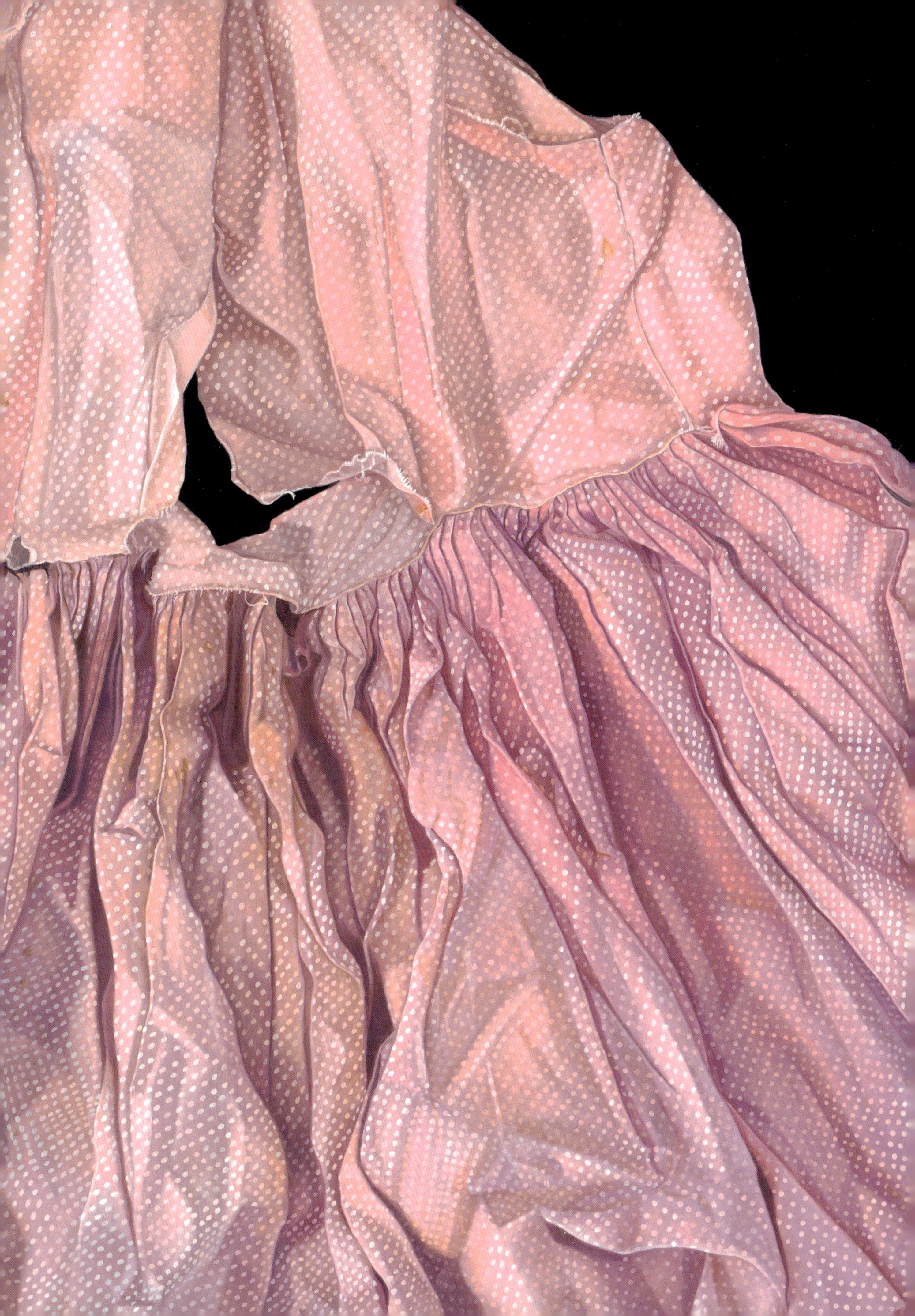

Mend Me, 2016

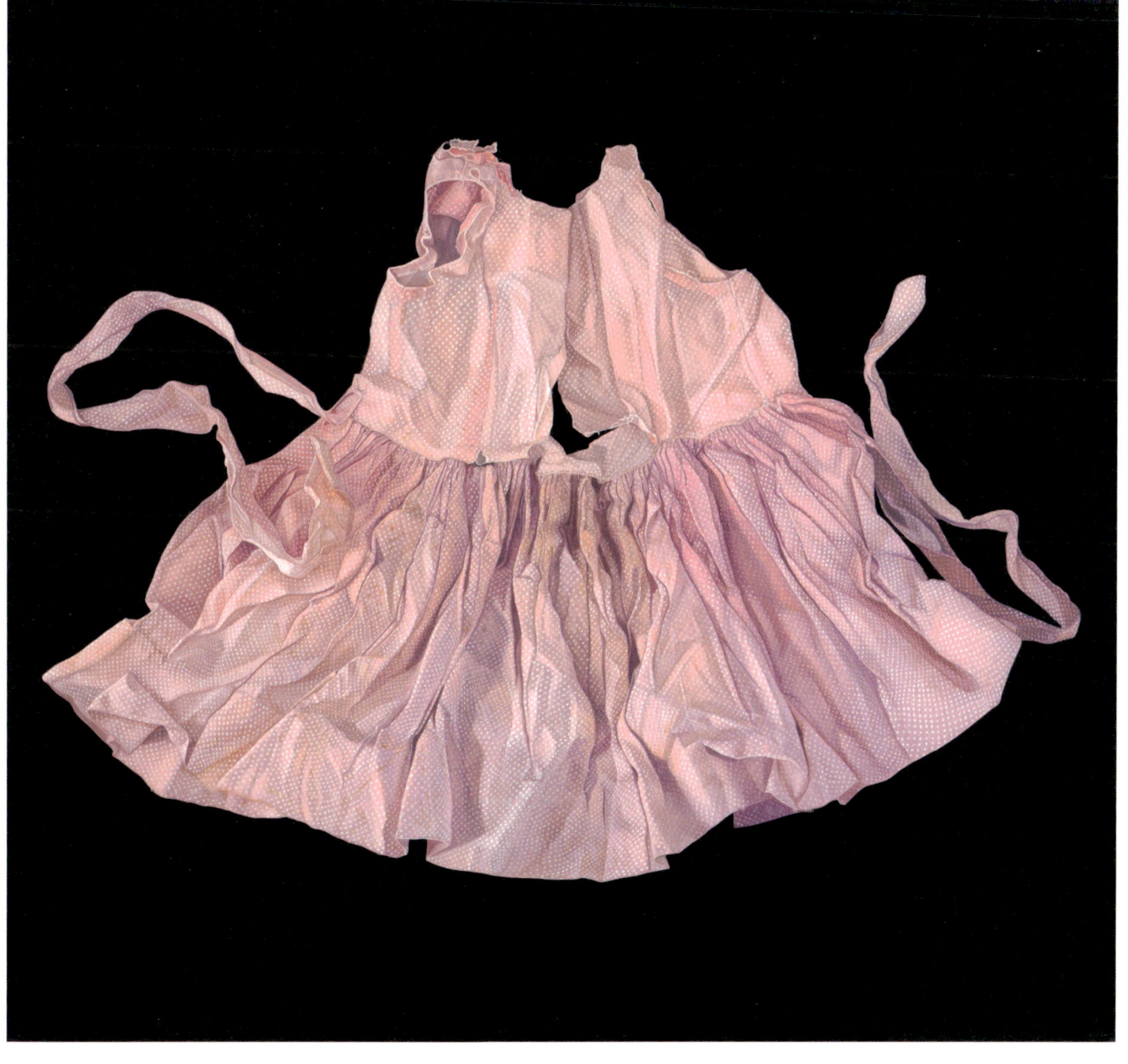

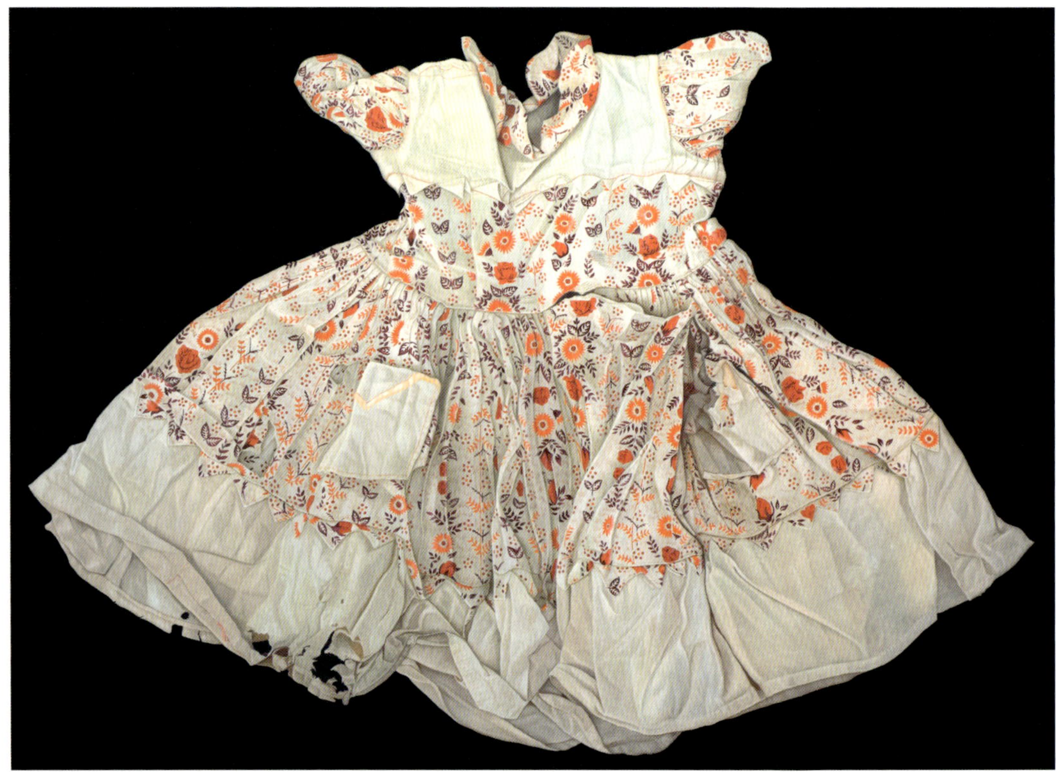

When Sonia Was Four (1958), 2017

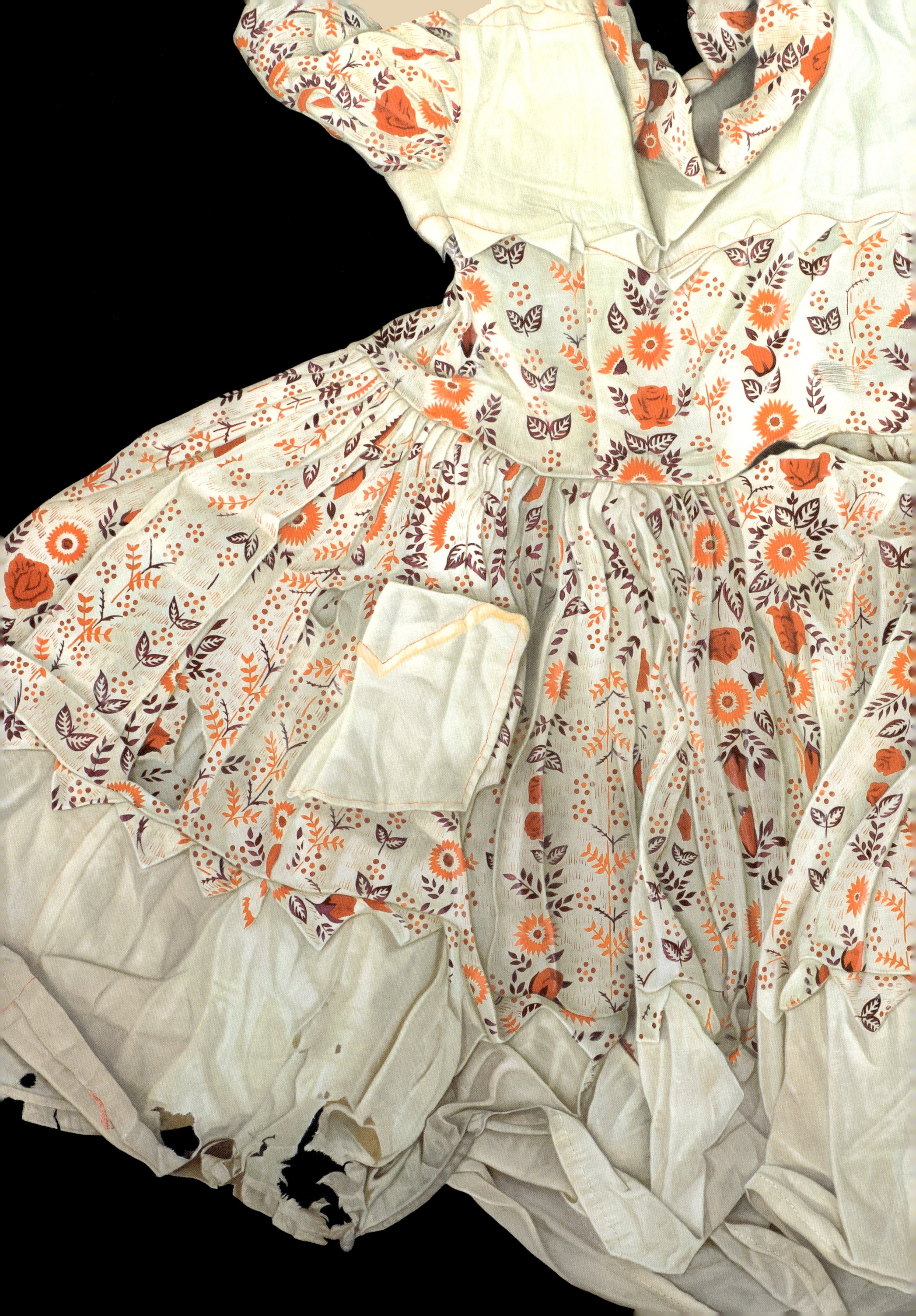

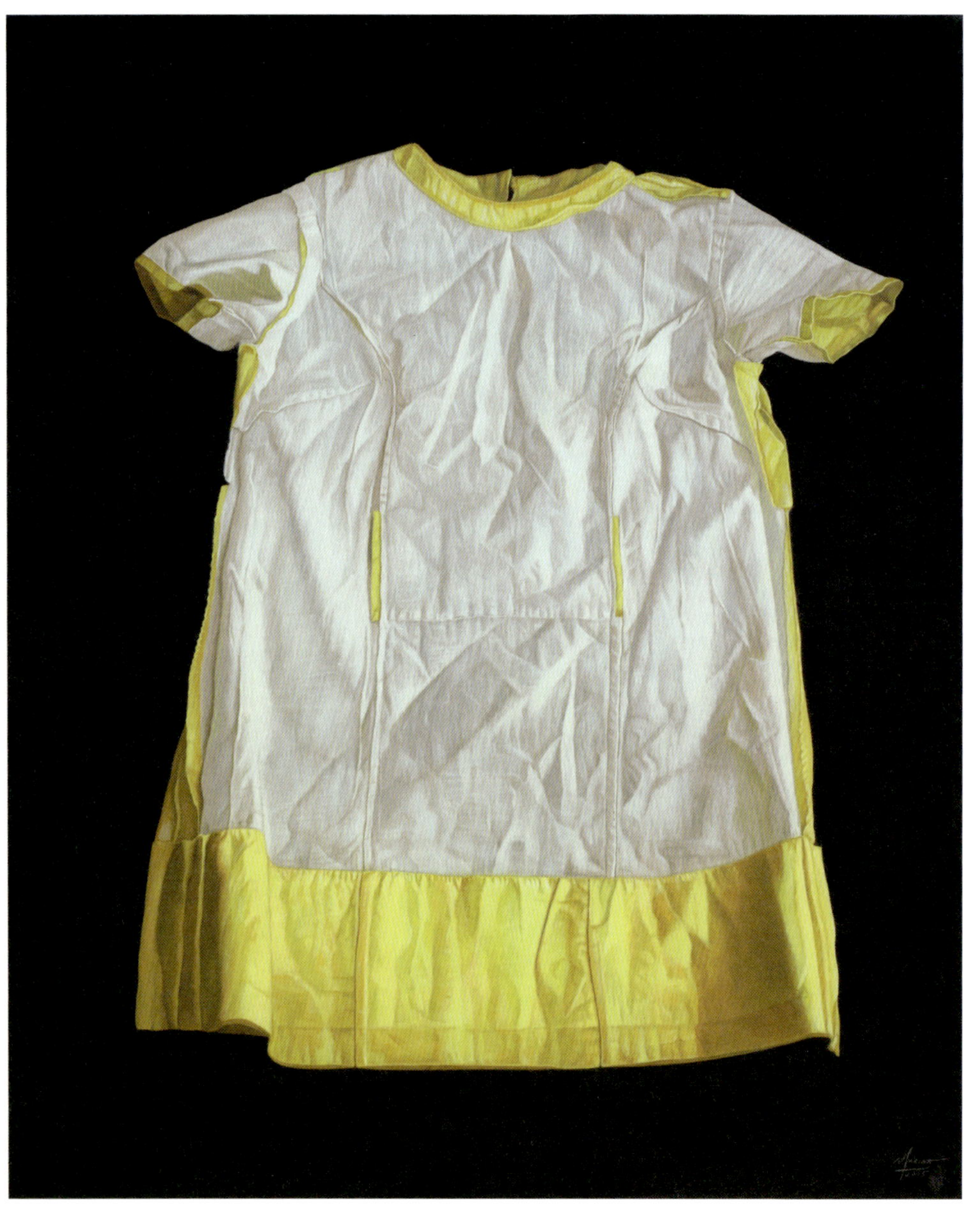

Meditations on White and Yellow Against Black, 2015

FOREWORD

Ever since I met Marina Cruz in her studio in the province of Bulacan near Manila in 2012, I have been fascinated by her work. Thus it is my great pleasure to present this book *Marina Cruz: Breathing Patterns*, which covers her most recent, substantial, and mature body of work, and which is being published subsequent to her first solo presentation in Germany (*Mend and Amends*, A3 Arndt Art Agency, Berlin, 2016/2017).

In Cruz's concept of working with the "absent" whilst weaving personal memories and stories into a multi-layered œuvre, I saw a kinship with the French artist Sophie Calle, with whom I have been working for many years. However, while Calle's work often revolves around her own autobiography, in Cruz´s work there is a celebration of the role of "mother"—or specifically, in this case, her grandmother. Cruz's artistic practice can be perceived as a personal homage to family, and in particular to the important role of the matriarch.

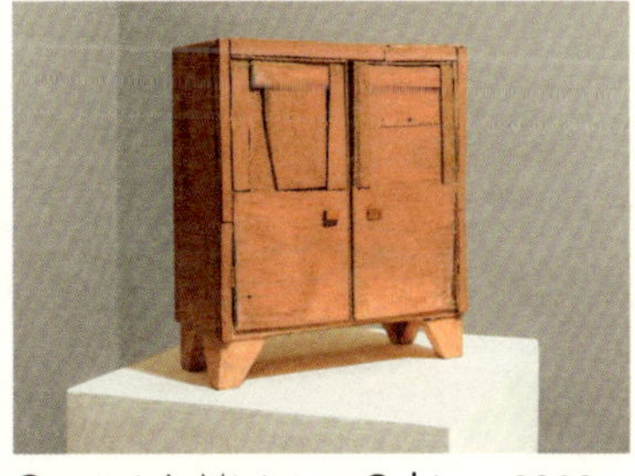

Gregorio's Miniature Cabinet, 2008

A few years ago, while searching for materials for another work, the artist came across dresses that had belonged to her mother and her aunt, sewed with great love by her grandmother when the twin girls were young, and later maintained, repaired, and stored in large cupboards. Since then it has been Cruz's artistic topic as well as her challenge to inventorize and meticulously paint the patterns and shapes of these textiles, into which the grandmother's handiwork is inscribed, along with the stories of their wearers and the passing of time. Like an archaeologist, she uncovers these telling traces in the rugged folds, diverse textures, and vibrant patterns of the garments.

On one hand her naturalistic painting of these real objects with a personal history demonstrates outstanding technical skills comparable to the Old Masters who, over centuries, proved their masterhood in depicting the most complex of draperies and textiles. On the other hand, Cruz's works also continue the legacy of abstract painting, as they depict the dresses from such close-up vantage points that they become unfamiliar to us and we are lured into reading them in abstract ways.

I would like to thank Marina Cruz for entrusting us with this collaboration. My gratitude also goes to the two authors—Kira Jürjens, whose essay examines the way in which the works are suspended between autobiographical narrative and formal reflexivity, and Philipp Bollmann, whose interview with the artist offers us a look behind the scenes.

Matthias Arndt

People share stories, but sometimes it appears that objects are the places where these stories dwell.[1]

Walter Benjamin, "Nachträge zu *Der Erzähler*"

SENSITIVE SURFACES TEXTILE IMAGERY IN THE PAINTINGS OF MARINA CRUZ

Kira Jürjens

1 Walter Benjamin, "Nachträge zu 'Der Erzähler,'" in Walter Benjamin, *Nachträge, Gesammelte Schriften*, vol. VII, part 2, eds. Rolf Tiedemann and Hermann Schweppenhäuser (Frankfurt am Main, 1989), p. 802.

Textiles are at the heart of Marina Cruz's work. They feature physically in her collages and installations, and are also the subject of her paintings and photographs. This focus on textiles occurred by chance: while searching for materials for another work, Cruz came across some dresses that had belonged to her mother and aunt when they were children. They were part of a collection of more than a hundred dresses that Cruz's grandmother had made for her twin daughters. This treasure trove of textiles has since formed the artistic core of Cruz's work, which is inspired by the stories "dwelling" in clothing—comparable to Walter Benjamin's observation in the quote above—and explores notions of family, ancestry, time, and memory. Through her work, Cruz transfers her grandmother's handiwork from the private family archive into the public realm of galleries and museums.

Cruz's art practice can be divided into different phases, based on the various perspectives from which the dresses are being examined. It is easy, therefore, to see how her work has developed: from a heavily archive-focused and narrative approach to a more formal and abstract one.[2] The **Inside/Out** (2012) series of text–image combinations, for example, looks at the relationship between the dresses and their wearers. Each of these works focuses on one dress and features a painting of the dress on canvas, a laminated photograph, and a quote embroidered on material. The embroideries bring an explicitly narrative element to the work, as they are stitched commentaries of those who once wore these dresses.[3]

2 Marina Cruz provides an overview of these individual phases in a conversation with the Mind Set Art Center. "Those come with time," [interview], in *Wear and Tear*, ed. Isabelle Kuo, exh. cat. Mind Set Art Center (Taiwan, 2015), pp. 55–59.

The almost analytical triptychons of the **Inside/Out** series feature photography, embroidery, and painting as individual elements, whereas more recent works consolidate all three media in single paintings: the fabric is reproduced in oil on canvas, from a photograph, and is the subject matter of the work rather than being materially present. These are the works discussed here.

While the dresses in **Inside/Out** are connected linguistically to their wearers by the embroidery, the artist moved away from such obvious story-telling in her later works. Instead, she began to concentrate more on the physical condition of the fabric—its stains, folds, and patterns—which she painted concentrating on color and texture. The explicitly autobiographical and narrative focus gave way to a more self-reflective, painterly approach.

While the stories dwelling in the objects are key in Cruz's work, how those stories are recorded, communicated, and presented is equally important. According to Benjamin, stories need to be shared by

3 The collage-like arrangement of these works was reminiscent of the embroidery samplers popular in Victorian England and created the impression that things were handmade when, in fact, the embroidery had been done by machine. For more on the embroidery technique in Cruz's work, see Thea Garing, "Wear and Tear", in ibid., pp. 17–21, here p. 19. On embroidery samplers, see Rozsika Parker, *The Subversive Stitch: Embroidery and the Making of the Feminine* (London, 1986). See also Anna Lehninger, "Embroidered Identity. Textile Autobiographies in Art Brut and Beyond," in *Metatextile: Identity and History of a Contemporary Art Medium*, ed. Tristan Weddigen (Emsdetten, 2010), pp. 41–50.

people—here, by the artist. In this respect, Cruz's work should be seen not just as an autobiographical take on the family archive but also as a fundamental reflection on how it can be represented. Marina Cruz's work will therefore be examined in this essay as an exploration of the possibilities and limitations of painterly representation in the context of three sets of antitheses: between the rather flat texture of surface and the pictorial space of the folds; between the presence and absence of the body; and between realism and abstraction.

The Aesthetic of the Surface and the Pictorial Space of the Clothes

In recent art-historical research, the portrayal of clothing and fabrics is no longer primarily analysed in terms of its symbolic meaning, nor as a historical index. Instead, the focus is on the physical properties of the material. In this approach, the fabric acquires significance as a means of artistic self-reflection.[4] The relationship between fabric and pictorial space is therefore particularly interesting. By definition, textiles are flat structures.[5] At the same time, however, they have the potential to be three-dimensional. In the delicate balance between surface and space, they are assigned a key importance in the history of modern art.[6] Traditionally, the plastic ductility of textiles was used in art primarily in relation to the modeling and representation of the body, or to showcase something behind or underneath the fabric that was hidden from view.[7] According to classicist art theory, drapery in sculpture served to show the movements and positions of the body, while in painting, since the Renaissance, its function has been to create the illusion of three-dimensional bodies. This changed in the 19th century when fabric increasingly disengaged from this functionalisation and acquired an aesthetic uniqueness in its flatness.[8] The fabric depicted in 20th-century art ultimately became one with the pictorial surface: the canvas is no longer imagined as a window to be looked through but is revealed in its own textility and becomes an object to be looked upon.

Marina Cruz's paintings must be viewed in the context of such a flattening of the pictorial space. For the most part, the fabrics in the more recent paintings fill the entire canvas and are arranged in parallel with the pictorial surface. Yet, despite the flatness of the fabrics depicted in these paintings, their naturalistic representation gives them a dimension of depth that is unique to them. The 2014 work **Chequered** (p. 7) shows an enlarged detail of a folded blue-and-white checked blouse with a snap fastener, which fills the entire frame of the canvas. The individual parts are difficult to identify in terms of their respective position and function in relation to the entire blouse. The squares on the material emphasise both the parallelity to the picture plane and the chessboard-like flatness.

At the same time, the image of the folded material conveys a depth of several millimetres, which can be gauged at the folded-back corner of the fabric in the top right-hand corner. The corner reveals the somewhat faded, slightly yellowed interior of the fabric. Below the snap fastener, in the middle of the picture, a narrow slit opens onto the dark interior of the dress. While the area where we see the fabric beneath exhibits a straightforward materiality and obstructs our view into deeper pictorial space, the dark slit conveys the hint of something

4 Michael Diers, "Mode im Bild, Modus des Bildes. Dargestellte Kleidung und die Selbstreflexion der Kunst," in *Kleidung im Bild. Zur Ikonologie dargestellter Gewandung*, ed. Philipp Zitzlsperger (Emsdetten, Berlin, 2010), pp. 195–211, here p. 195.

5 See also Monika Wagner, Dietmar Rübel, Sebastian Hackenschmidt (eds.), *Lexikon des künstlerischen Materials. Werkstoffe der modernen Kunst von Abfall bis Zinn* (Munich, 2002).

6 An exhibition in the Kunstmuseum Wolfsburg recently alluded to the importance of textiles in modern art: Markus Brüderlin, "Introduction to the exhibition: The birth of abstraction from the spirit of the textile and the conquest of the fabric space," in *Art & Textiles Fabric as Material and Concept in Modern Art from Klimt to the Present*, ed. Markus Brüderlin, exh. cat. Kunstmuseum Wolfsburg (2013/2014), Staatsgalerie Stuttgart (2014), Ostfildern (2013), pp. 14–45. For more on this subject, see also Joseph Masheck, "The Carpet Paradigm. Critical Prolegomena to a Theory of Flatness," in *Arts Magazine*, no. 51/1 (September 1976), pp. 82–109.

7 For a thorough investigation of the subject, see also Gerhard Wolf, *Schleier und Spiegel. Traditionen des Christus-Bildes und die Bildkonzepte der Renaissance* (Munich, 2002).

8 See also Claudia Blümle, "Das Bild als Vorhang," in *Hinter dem Vorhang. Verhüllung und Enthüllung seit der Renaissance – von Tizian bis Christo*, eds. Claudia Blümle and Beat Wismer, exh. cat. Kunstpalast Düsseldorf (Munich, 2016), pp. 30–39, here p. 38.

hidden. This duality is reminiscent of the traditional imagery of the curtain with its function as a threshold between metaphysical backworlds and a material presence.[9] Yet—and this is how Marina Cruz's approach differs from the traditional curtain motif—this hidden element lies not behind but rather in the folds of the dress.

9 Ibid.

Empty Shell and Second Skin: Absence and Presence

Marina Cruz's paintings of clothes, which fill the pictorial space, contain no depictions of the human body. The fabric does not purport to evoke an underlying, three-dimensional body. Nor does it seek to embed the wearer in an external reference system of social identifying marks. Nevertheless, the fabric relates closely to the human body in its pictorial uniqueness. The portrayal of the clothes appears as a reflection on the conditions and possibilities of representation, through which absence is realised.

Speaking in an interview, Marina Cruz recalls the moment when she found the dresses that her mother wore as a child. She was particularly struck by the realisation that her mother had once been so small.[10] Using the difficulty of imagining her mother's body during childhood as a starting point, Cruz produces works that revolve around what might best be expressed as the "vacancy" of the body. The exploration of the absent body based on the materially present fabric can be explained by looking at **Red and White Stripes** (2014) (p. 15). Using the finest brushstrokes, red and white longitudinal stripes are painted on a dress that is turned inside out. The dress's ruffled skirt spreads out to the edges of the painting. Running through the middle of the picture, from the top left to the lower middle, a glimpse is provided into the inner lining of the bust area. The visible seams and hems expose the material construction of the dress. The composition also draws the eye to the center of the painting, into the dark interior of the dress, which remains hidden from view. In this work, the dress is not covering an underlying human body, but the evocative drapery with its flesh- and skin-like coloring definitely gives the dress itself a physical dimension. The fabric, "a second skin," acts as a metonym for the absent body of the wearer. The mother's body is draped here as the "origin of the world,"[11] as it were.

10 Marina Cruz in conversation on the occasion of her solo exhibition *Mend and Amends*, A3 Arndt Art Agency, Berlin, 2016/2017 in Rachael Vance, *Material Inspiration*, December 5, 2016, https://arndtartagency.wordpress.com/2016/12/05/a3-editorial-marina-cruz-2/, accessed March 7, 2017.

11 This expression refers to Gustave Courbet's *L'Origine du Monde* (1866), which portrays the female lower abdomen and genitalia in explicit, close-up detail. In Cruz's painting this association is only hinted at.

In other works the scuffs, discolorations, and stains also refer to the absent body. The traces of previous contact between the body and the fabric tell stories of the wearers of the clothes. In **Stains and Shadows** (2014) (p. 13), we see the formerly white inner lining of a dress. The hem at the top right edge of the picture provides a glimpse of the blue-gray-brown pattern of the outside of the dress. The threads have loosened on the seam that runs vertically through the center of the painting. The horizontal darts in the inner lining meet the vertical seam in the middle of the picture and together they form a grid-like structure. In the bottom third of the painting, parallel to the darts, is a shadowy crease, a few centimeters wide, which is probably due to the way the dress was folded and stored. One large and two small reddish-brown, dried-in stains can also be distinguished in the bottom third of the painting. Even if the wound that produced these bloodstains has healed long ago, it is still preserved as an "injury" to the fabric of the dress.

With its stains and dark patches, the fabric here seems to be a delicate surface on which the traces of use emerge as a type of picture within a picture. The depiction of fabric, which in a broader sense is itself a picture support, suggests a reference to the pictorial tradition of the *vera ikon*,[12] in the sense that an absent body presents itself in the stain.[13] Unlike the Veil of Veronica, however, the bodily fluids absorbed by the fabrics do not coagulate into a referential image. Moreover, the fabric in its staging as an object containing trace material is not used for religious devotion but rather for the artistic investigation of a private family archive. However, the fabric depicted in these works does share one thing with the vera ikon and—reflecting a classical concept of photographic theory—with the photograph: the trace-like character that testifies to a former presence.[14] It is the small, everyday stories that are, seemingly automatically, reflected in the texture of the fabric just as in the light-sensitive surface of the photograph.[15] The fabrics in the paintings therefore act as documents of the past and an index of time.[16] Unlike photography, Marina Cruz's works deal with the representation of traces, which must not be confused with the trace itself. The trace by definition is coincidental, while Cruz's representation is deliberately made.[17] As painted traces, the stains and folds in Marina Cruz's works gain a formal aesthetic function by shaping the structure of the painting and the composition of color. The painterly transformation of the imperfect stain into a constituent component of the composition is also revealing in terms of the tradition of the representation of textiles.

While Cruz reproduces the details of the various textures with a precision seen in the Dutch *fijnschilderei*[18] of the 17th century, her approach differs fundamentally from the treatment of textiles at that time. Instead of the gleaming integrity and stiff crispness of the fabrics in the paintings of a Gerard ter Borch (1617–1681) or a Frans van Mieris the Elder (1635–1681), Marina Cruz's fabrics appear in their age-related threadbareness with stains and injuries. For Cruz, the fabric is no longer bound up in the avoidance of disgust—an aesthetic strategy evoked particularly in Classicism.[19] In the discussion on clothing in sculpture from Johann Joachim Winckelmann (1717–1768) to Georg Wilhelm Friedrich Hegel (1770–1831), clothes on the body played a part in "extinguish[ing] [...] its little veins, wrinkles, little hairs on the head."[20] The fabric was designed to create an ideal and intact surface that guaranteed the beauty of the artwork.

The clothing fabrics portrayed by Marina Cruz are far removed from the intact, transparent garments of the idealistic, classicist aesthetic. As utilitarian objects, they have absorbed the traces of their wearers and their environment and are subject to progressive disintegration.

There is a certain ruthlessness in the level of detail with which the paintings reproduce the loose threads, the holes, and the stains. Yet these random components, which threaten the cohesion of the dress and impair its functionality in the real-world context, have a right of their own in the painting. They hold the composition together. They have a formal stake in the visual effect and, in their level of detail, illustrate Cruz's technical skill. The pictures are thus incorporated into a dialectic movement: the dysfunctionality of the everyday world seen in the discarded and rejected utilitarian object acquires an aesthetic function in the course of its transfer to the image.

12 On the subject of the image of the *vera ikon*, see Gerhard Wolf's overview "Vera icon," in *Handbuch der Bildtheologie in vier Bänden*, ed. Reinhard Hoeps, vol. 3 (Paderborn, Munich, 2014), pp. 419–466.

13 On the history of pictures that "make themselves," see Friedrich Weltzien, *Fleck. Das Bild der Selbsttätigkeit* (Göttingen, 2011).

14 For more on the impact of the vera ikon in relation to photography theory, see Gerhard Wolf, "'In principio velum', am Anfang war das Tuch: Raphaelle Peales 'Venus rising from the sea: a deception' und die Bildtradition der 'vera icon'," in Blümle, Wismer 2016 (see note 8), pp. 132–141, here p. 134. Rosalind Krauss sees the photographic "as the ultimate locale of the trace," Rosalind Krauss, "Tracing Nadar," in October 5 (Summer 1978), pp. 29–47, here p. 45.

15 The paintings also relate to photography by virtue of how they are made: each painting is based on a photograph that Cruz uses as a template for the painting.

16 Yet, unlike photography, which records individual moments, the clothes represent stages of life. It is not the standout moment but the continuing passage of time that becomes visible in the well-worn and torn fabrics in the paintings.

17 See also Sybille Krämer, "Was also ist eine Spur? Und worin besteht ihre epistemologische Rolle? Eine Bestandsaufnahme," in *Spur. Spurenlesen als Orientierungstechnik und Wissenskunst*, eds. Sybille Krämer, Werner Kogge, and Gernot Grube (Frankfurt am Main, 2007), pp. 11–33, here p. 16.

18 This Dutch term for "fine painting" refers particularly to the Leiden school, which was noted for its meticulously detailed still lifes, portraits, and genre scenes. In order to achieve the high degree of detail and the resulting illusionistic effects, the painters often used panels of wood or copper as supports because, unlike canvas, these supports did not affect the appearance of the painting with any structure. See also Linda Stone-Ferrier, *Images of Textiles. The Weave of Seventeenth-Century Dutch Art and Society* (Ann Arbor, 1980).

19 Winfried Menninghaus, *Ekel. Theorie und Geschichte einer starken Empfindung* (Frankfurt am Main, 1999).

20 Georg Wilhelm Friedrich Hegel, "The Ideal of Sculpture," in Georg Wilhelm Friedrich Hegel, *Aesthetics: Lectures on Fine Art*, vol. 2 (Oxford, 1975). Quoted in https://www.marxists.org/reference/archive/hegel/works/ae/part3-section2.htm, accessed March 15, 2017.

Close-Up Views: Ornament and Abstraction

Marina Cruz's works can be seen as her attempt to approximate her origins. The visual representation corresponds with this process: the temporal distance to the past that cannot be recovered is contrasted with the representation from the greatest possible spatial proximity and in microscopic enlargement. The traces, stains, tears, and injuries are reproduced with forensic accuracy.[21] In doing so, no light spots or highlights designed to produce meaning, which would hierarchically organise the pictorial surface, are included. The fabrics are evenly lit; each detail is executed with the same importance. Even though every loose thread and every threadbare spot is made visible, the entire whole and its context remain invisible: the paintings acquire an abstract dimension precisely in their naturalistic attention to detail. It is the proximity that makes the everyday object of a worn dress alien to us.

21 For more on the epistemic character of the index paradigm, see Carlo Ginzburg, "Spurensicherung. Der Jäger entziffert die Fährte, Sherlock Holmes nimmt die Lupe, Freud liest Morelli – Die Wissenschaft auf der Suche nach sich selbst," in Carlo Ginzburg, *Spurensicherung. Die Wissenschaft auf der Suche nach sich selbst* (Berlin, 2002), pp. 61–96.

This is particularly evident in the works featuring brightly colored, printed fabrics. In **Just balls, and atoms, and planets, and a hole** (2015, pp. 61–63), the pattern, which is reminiscent of an abstract ball of wool, has its own pictorality. The human body is completely absent from this stain-free dress. This particular dress has less draping, and is neatly folded. The planar pattern on the fabric, whose colorfulness stands out clearly from the white background of the dress, corresponds to the flatness of the cloth's arrangement. The representational portrayal of the dress is thus subordinate to the ornamental abstraction of the "balls," "planets," or "atoms" dominating the pictorial surface. A hole in the middle of the picture reveals the underlying layer of fabric with the same pattern. Differentiated only by a slight shadowing from the overlying layer, the pattern below moves to the fore in its colorfulness so there is not much distinction between the two layers. Here, in contrast to earlier works, the hole does not provide a view into the interior of the dress but instead presents another, outer side to see. The staged inspection does not give rise to a spatial dimension of depth but to an equally opaque and ornamental fabric. Thus the artist presents the dress to the viewer as another support on the textile support of the canvas. In this exploration of the flatness of both the support medium and the subject of the picture, the artist reflects on the history of abstraction that is closely linked to the textile ornament.[22] However, Marina Cruz's work amounts to more than the self-reflexive gesture of painting. With her paintings she also preserves the fragmented documents of her own family history, and enters into a dialogue with both the handicraft of her grandmother and the childhood of her mother and aunt. She shares the stories dwelling in the "injured" clothes by translating the stitches into brushstrokes.

22 This context was last explored in an exhibition in the Fondation Beyeler. See also *Ornament and Abstraction, The Dialogue Between Non-Western, Modern and Contemporary Art*, ed. Markus Brüderlin, exh. cat. Fondation Beyeler (Cologne, 2002). On the significant influence of textiles on abstraction in modern art, see Brüderlin 2013 (see note 6), pp. 14–45.

SUBTLE HISTORIES A CONVERSATION WITH MARINA CRUZ

Philipp Bollmann

Philipp Bollmann Recently you presented paintings from your current body of work in a solo exhibition at Arndt Art Agency, Berlin. The motifs of all these works were dresses or pieces of clothing, and the title of the show was *Mend and Amends*. Could you say something about the title and the underlying theme of the exhibition?

Marina Cruz The title is a play of words and ideas. "To mend" means to make something broken usable again. Usually it's a term used when one repairs or stitches together the damaged parts of a dress. "To amend" means to improve, change, modify or simply reframe something, to enable us to look at it in new ways. But besides these literal definitions I also had in mind more abstract meanings. The word "amend" implies forgiving, healing or curing something: perhaps a relationship or a negative emotion. And in this sense it refers to a very personal level: I was working on this body of work at a time when my late grandmother was very weak, fragile and bedridden due to old age and Alzheimer's. My mom and I took care of her. She was a strong woman, a widow for thirty years, and the maker of the dresses depicted in the paintings; she's the matriarch and the backbone of the family, yet she was worn out and waiting to rest. It's almost surreal to see a strong figure like her weaken before your very eyes. She passed away around the time of the completion of these works. So it was like a symbolic transition to mend the relationship and cherish the past, and acknowledge that our vulnerabilities and brokenness are part of life, part of who we are.

PB But dresses with a history—in your case a personal one—as motifs seem to have interested you for a much longer period of time.

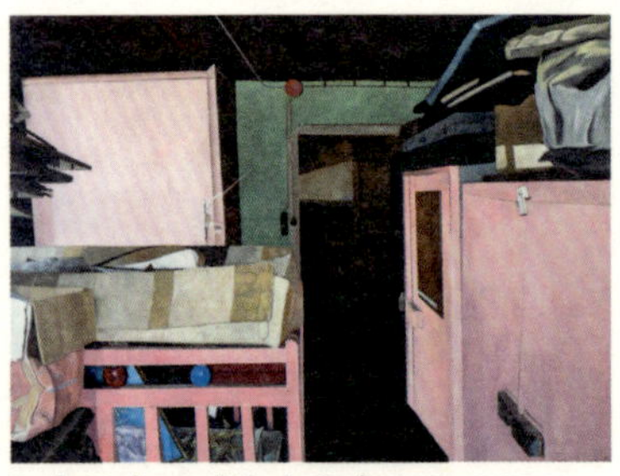

Pink Crib and Pink Cabinets, 2017

MC When I was young, about nine years of age, I wanted to become an archaeologist, unearthing relics, or a palaeontologist discovering fossils. Well, I didn't go to a desert or a site full of those but I found myself looking into things, objects in my grandmother's house, particularly the dresses. Dresses are very ordinary objects, yet behind their banality and mundane qualities are accounts of subtle histories, both biographical and cultural. The meanings lie in the personal narratives attached to the dresses. The dresses became a starting point for a conversation, a subtle way of getting to know, inquiring and revealing details in a personal archive. It was like an urge to look for something, even if I didn't know what I was looking for. Maybe this urge came from a promise my late grandfather made to me before my birthday; he said he would give me a surprise. As a young girl I was very excited about the present but the next day, on my birthday, my grandfather passed away and I never found out what his gift for me was.

PB Besides these autobiographical aspects, your work also refers to more universal issues. Clothing in our days is usually no longer oriented to longevity. Fashion trends that are rapidly followed around the globe seem to be more important than individuality. In light of this your work pleads for a different view, by drawing attention to the fact that clothes are an expression of both cultural and regional identity, and serve as a preservation medium of not only cultural but also very personal histories.

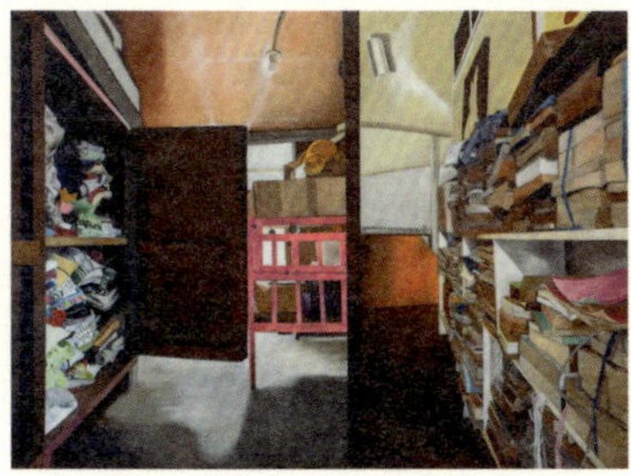
Personal Archive I and II, 2017

MC Yes, but I also want to draw attention to the fact that back then those clothes were made, not bought. People had time to make their clothes and they made them not just for a hobby but also for pragmatic reasons. There was a strong tradition of tailoring clothes for one's own family. It was very interesting to me to find out that some of the materials used in dressmaking during the 1950s and 1960s were chicken-feed packaging. My grandfather took care of a few chickens, and my grandmother would upcycle these sack materials by creating tiny prints and patterns on them; she would then make children's dresses out of them. Today there is a global commodification and overproduction, while back then there was a frugal and careful, mindful creation of clothes.

PB So could one say your work is also an homage to the art of tailoring? I see some parallels between sewing a dress and painting on a formal level as both deal with colors, patterns, lines, and shapes. This parallel is echoed in your paintings as their compositions are very much defined by the interplay of the stitched lines and sewn folds as well as the patterns and colors of the actual dress.

MC Yes, I am very interested in the formal qualities of the dresses and they inspire me. But when choosing a motif, I look for something interesting: this doesn't necessarily have to be a visual quality; it can also, for example, be a haptic one. When I hold a piece of clothing, I let it speak to me, I feel, smell and see the material, colors, patterns, textures, folds, and creases, and also the imperfections of the objects: the stains, tears, and blemishes. To me these dresses are like "still lifes".

Sometimes I depict a whole dress in a macro view, or just an interesting detail in a micro view. This process is enjoyable; to reframe, to crop, to emphasize, to create some mystery, to force the viewer to look more closely, and in a different way, at the garments.

PB I see what you mean by "mystery." Especially those works presenting a "micro view"—as you call it—of a dress are somehow puzzling, as their reading oscillates between trompe-l'oeil and abstraction.

MC Yes, I'm fascinated by abstraction, by the enjoyment of elements and forms. Even though my reference is a representational subject such as fabric, I like the fact that I can look into it through different lenses—in representational or non-representational ways. And there is some magic or poetry when a material such as fabric is depicted in a larger-than-life way; I like that.

PB The element of imperfection is very present in your paintings. The dresses show traces of use and spots of dirt. Some colors are faded out. So you also make visible the passing of time and the unknown history of both the dresses and their wearers.

MC Yes, maybe because the subject matter, the clothes, is really a witness of the past, and that they were worn by people who have already aged. And, yes, by acknowledging the imperfections there is an acceptance of the past and a kind of celebration of the blemishes, as the clothes get more beautiful with age.

PB Would you go so far as to declare your paintings as portraits?

MC Yes, portraits without wearers. I like the mystery and anonymity of the people who used to own and wear this clothing like a second, chosen skin.

PB The painting quality is stunning. Some layers of paint are very thin, so the structure of the canvas shines through and unites beautifully with the subtle brushstrokes. At the same time one is lured into mistaking the texture of the canvas for the texture of the cloth depicted. A great effect! Your paintings are almost photorealist, yet they have a very strong tactile quality.

MC I hope to let the viewer experience the sensual qualities of painting, but I don't claim my work to be like photorealist painting, because the brushstrokes are still visible. But yes, it's one of my aims to allow a viewer to experience the tactile qualities of paint and the subject depicted.

PB Chuck Close (* 1940) or Franz Gertsch (* 1930), for example, are very famous colleagues from another generation, who pointed the way regarding photorealistic painting in post-war contemporary art. Even though you said you don't consider yourself as a photorealistic painter, have these artists—or any others—had an influence on your work?

MC Actually, no.

PB But like the photorealists, you paint your grandmother's handmade dresses from photographs, right?

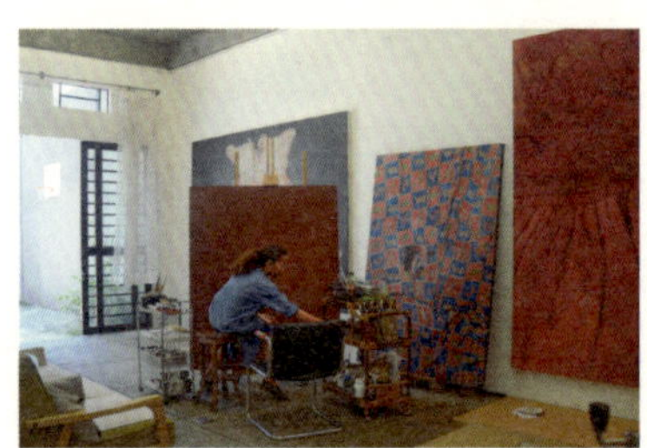

Marina Cruz in her studio

MC Yes, photography helps me to frame, to divide into sections and segments, and allows me to concentrate on small details, dissecting them into tones, colors, textures. But I also have the actual dress on hand for reference to actual textures and other features.

I suppose if I had to name any artistic influences, I would instead mention the works of Antonio López García (* 1936).

PB You mean the Spanish Realist?

MC Right. I saw his retrospective show at the Museum of Fine Arts in Boston, in 2008. Back then I wasn't yet painting clothing; I was just doing collographs using fabric and photographs of dresses; I had the photographs printed on canvas and then embroidered them. But that exhibition may have had an impact on me since it made me recall the sheer joy of painting.

PB The Spanish colonial period was very defining for the cultural identity of your country. Might this be a reason why you feel so strongly connected to Spanish art?

MC Yes, the Spanish colonial period lasted for 300 years and as a child going to church every week, growing up with murals and paintings about Christianity, plus stained-glass windows, statues of saints and religious sculptures or icons, I came to have a strong sense of its influence on my pictorial perceptions. In the Philippines we learn religion through images and pictures; maybe that's why Filipino art is so strong in representation.

PB You studied painting at the University of the Philippines in Quezon City. Was the formal training you gained there representational in style?

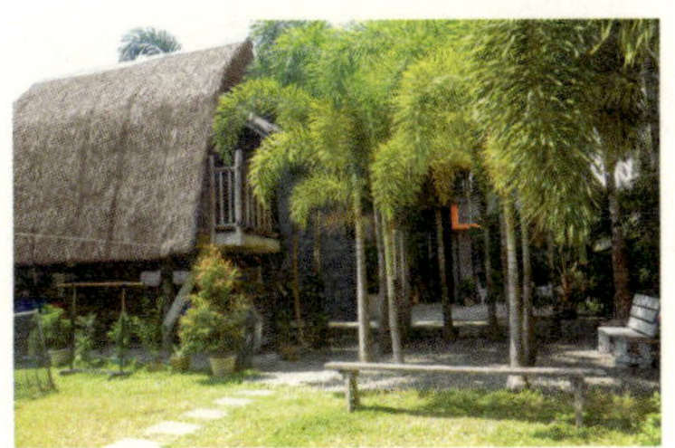
Studio of Marina Cruz in Bulacan

MC It was an exciting time for me. We had professors with differing ways of teaching: some leaning more towards the conceptual school of thought, some stronger on indigenous influences, and others focusing on forms and elements. I think I had a very good training from the University of the Philippines; the painting exercises were very challenging and required many hours to fulfil, which was a good foundation for enduring lengthy processes and really working hard. We were taught painting techniques that greatly helped us to learn to mix colors and to employ drawing devices to improve hand and eye coordination. However, even more than the formalistic training, it was also a great time to develop your concepts and voice. There was a pool of great mentors whom you could ask for advice; they might have ridiculed your work, at times, but they also helped you polish not just your craft but your ideas. And there was also a good sense of competition due to seeing other students on higher levels doing excellent work.

PB Recently, Matthias Arndt organized the exhibitions *Wasak! Filipino Art Today* (Berlin, 2015) and *Chimères: Visions of South East Asia* (Paris, 2016, in cooperation with Hervé Mikaeloff). How do you see yourself connected to the artists whose works were presented alongside yours in these exhibitions? Do you have any kind of intellectual exchange?

MC In terms of connections, here in the Philippines artists tend to know each other and there is a mutual respect. Intellectual exchanges happen rarely, maybe only during talks at art fairs or exhibitions. My husband Rodel Tapaya and I live and work in the province of Bulacan, and we seldom go to Manila except for very important events.

PB How would you describe the current art scene in the Philippines?

MC There's still a lot to be done. But I think it's getting more attention now compared to about ten years ago. There are more exhibition venues now and the existing spaces are expanding. The Filipino art scene that is emerging is exciting; it's growing, developing, and becoming more thought-provoking. People of all ages but especially the young people are beginning to get curious and want to learn more about art—and that's a very good sign.

The interview was conducted in January 2017 via email.

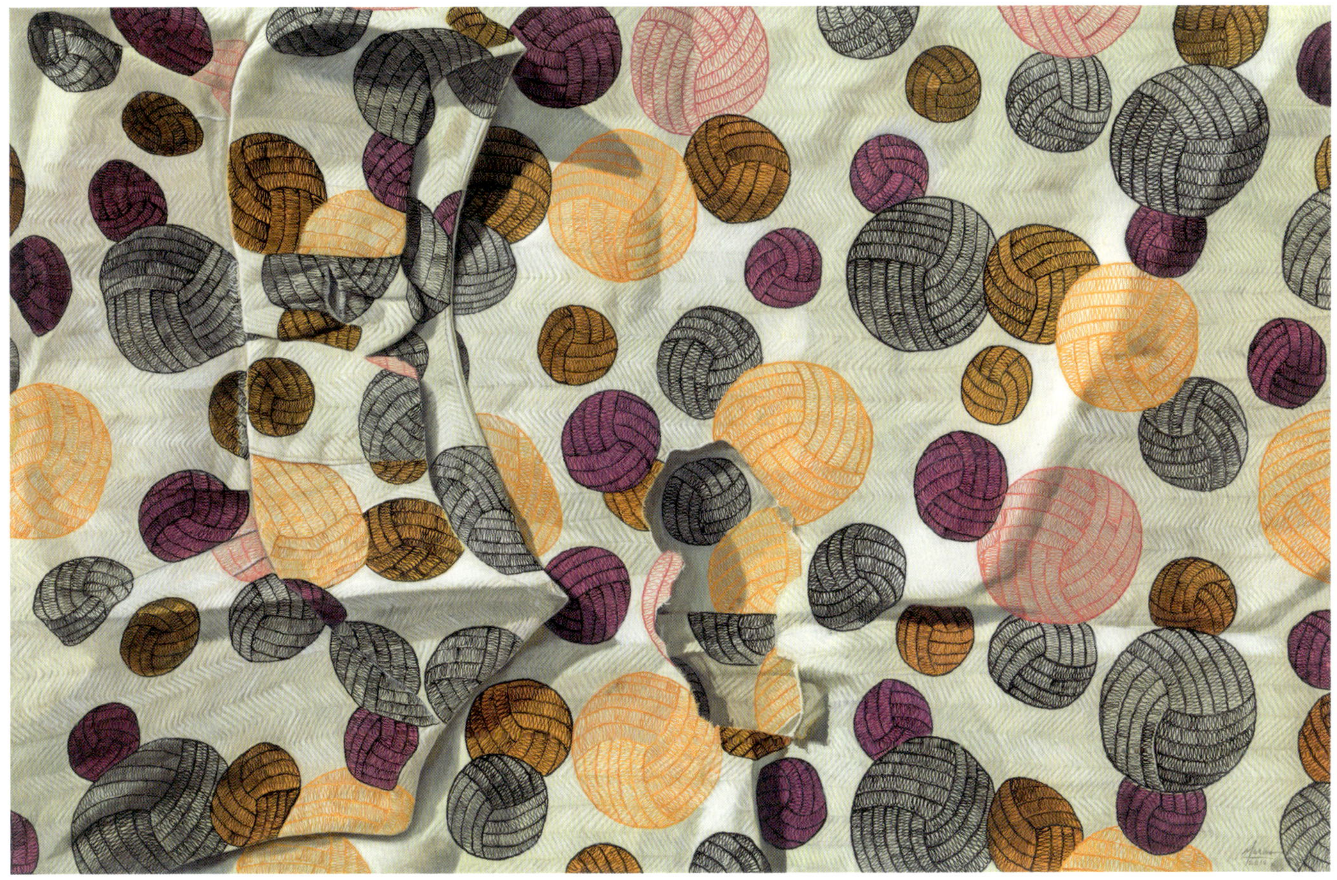

Just balls, and atoms, and planets, and a hole, 2015

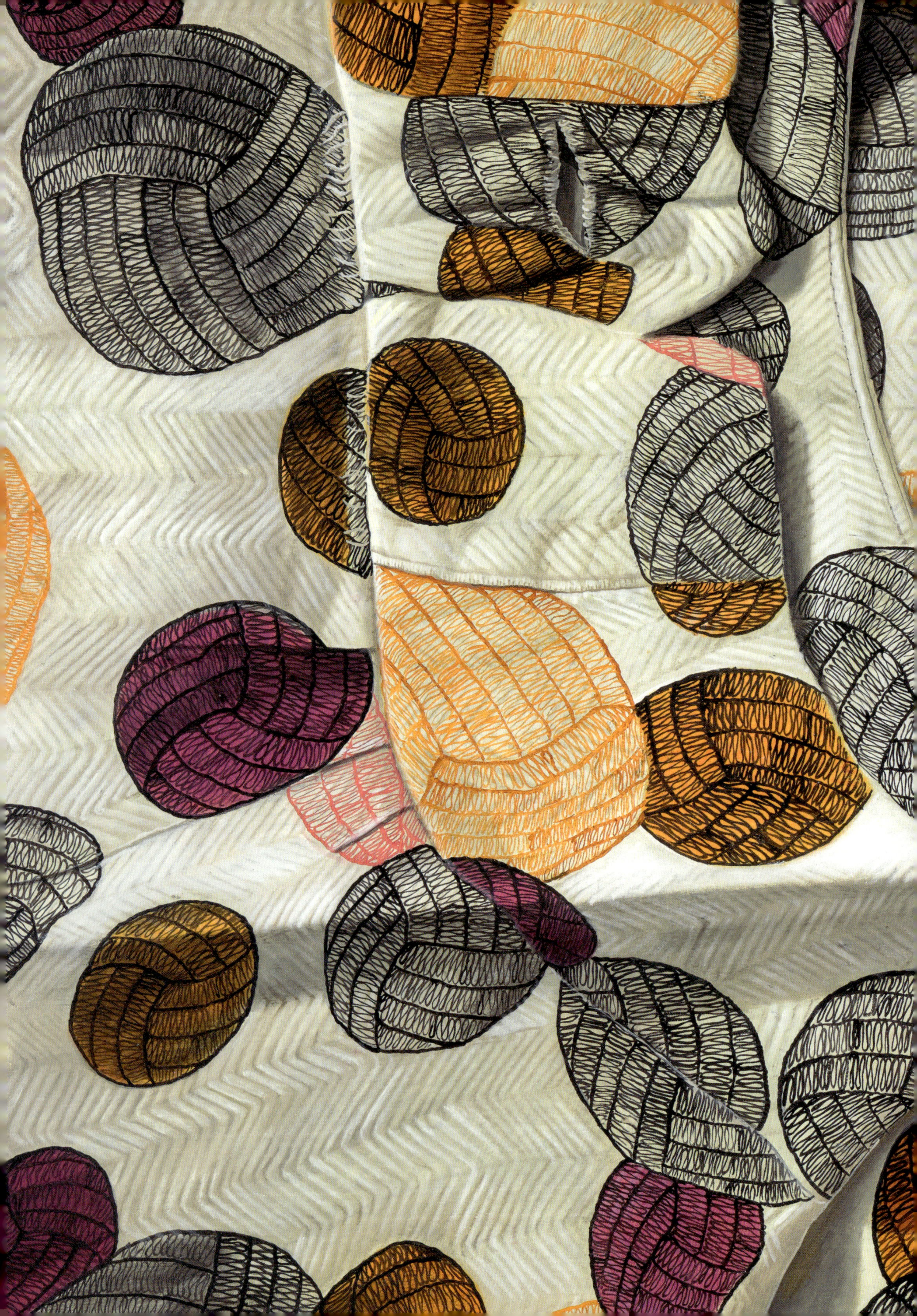

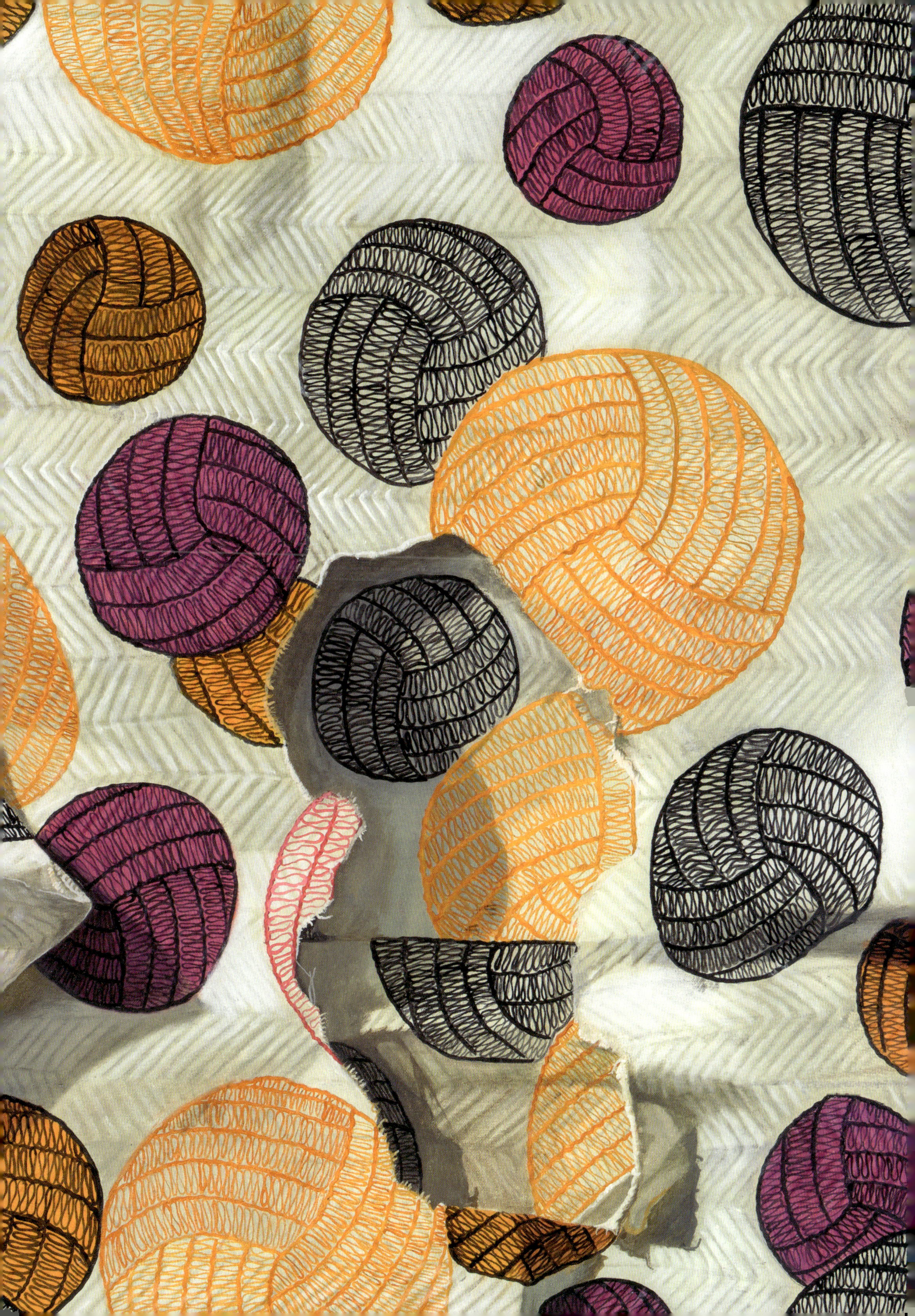

Intertwining Rings and Threads, 2016

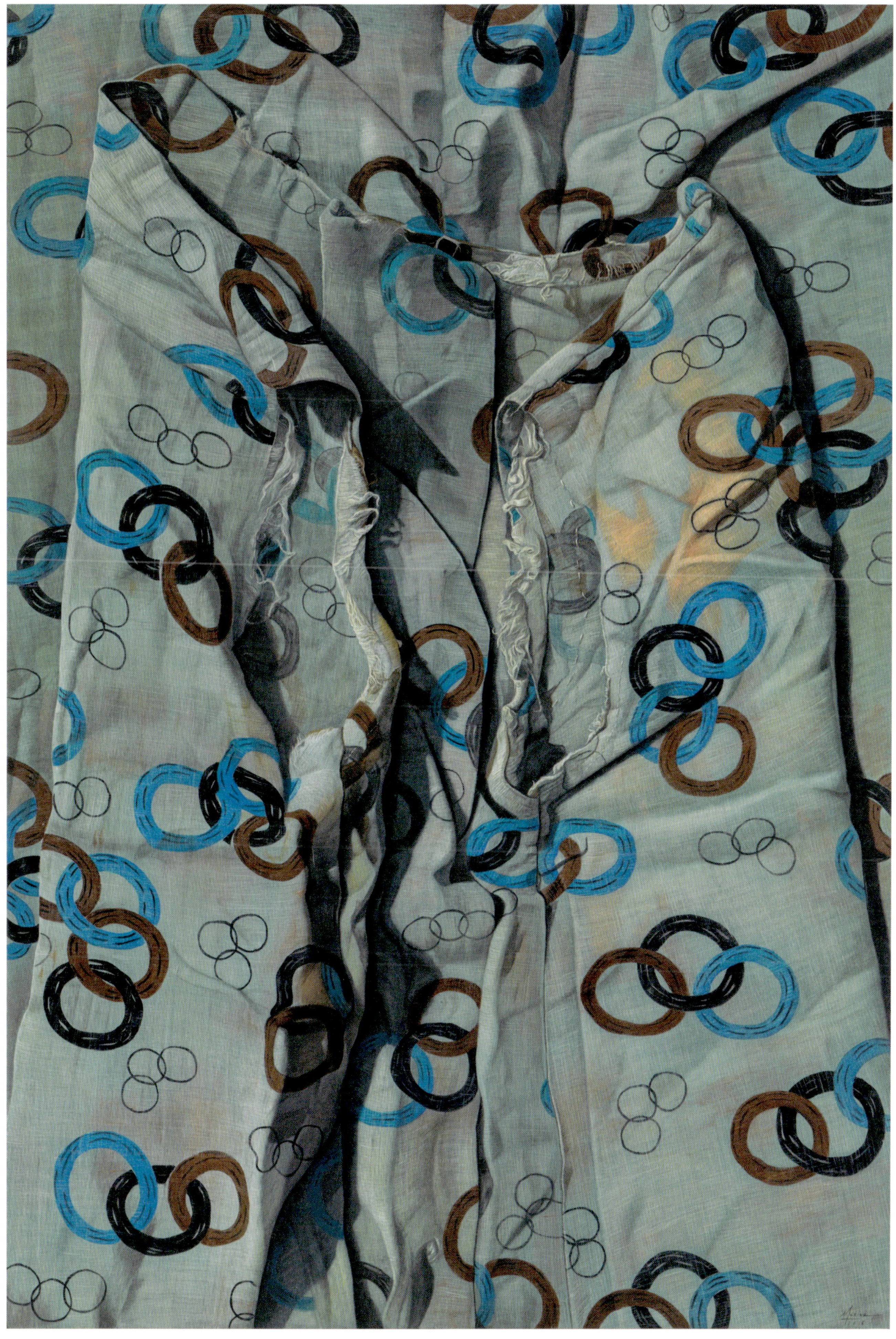

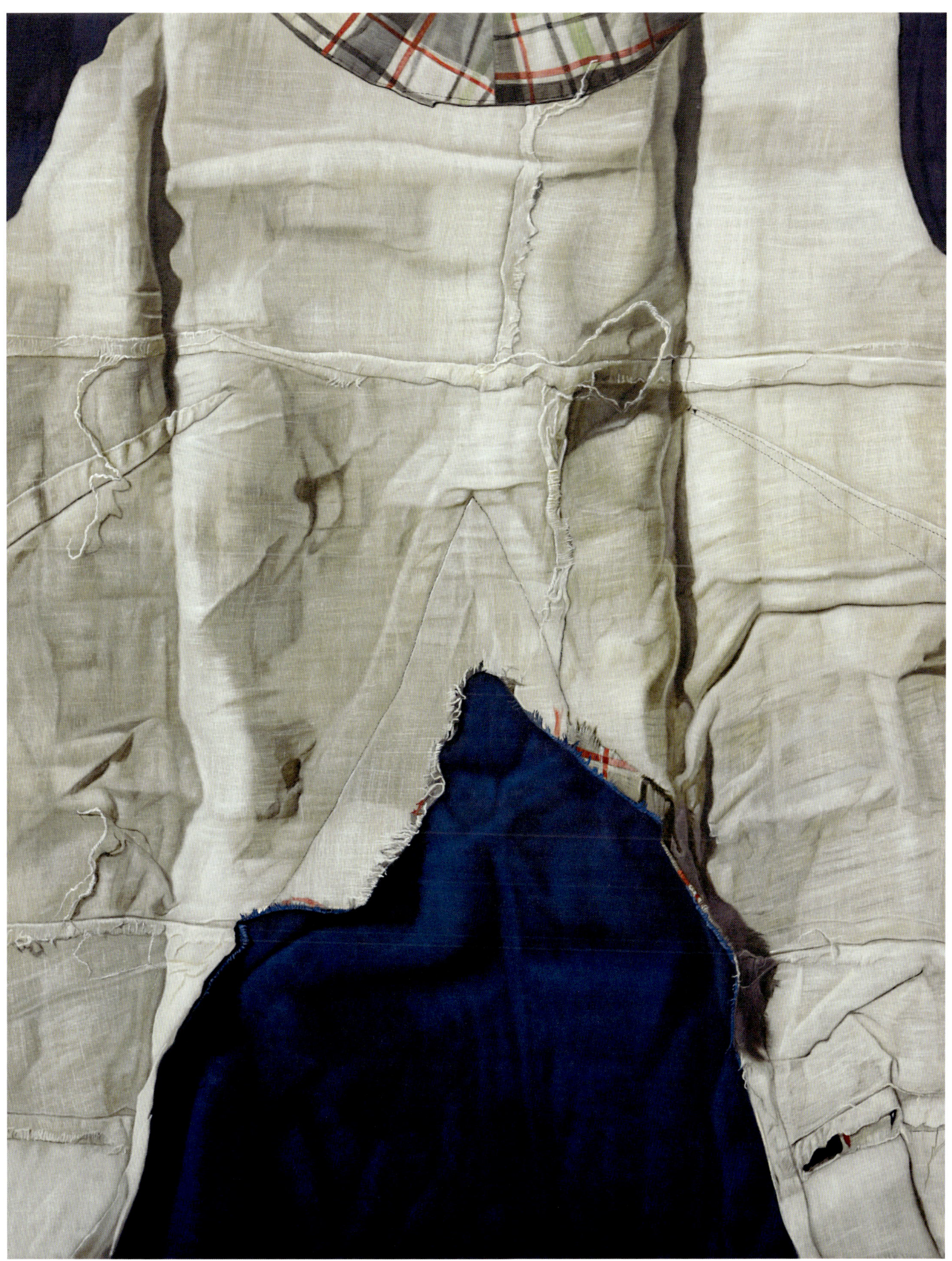

Blue Mountain Against White Skies, 2016

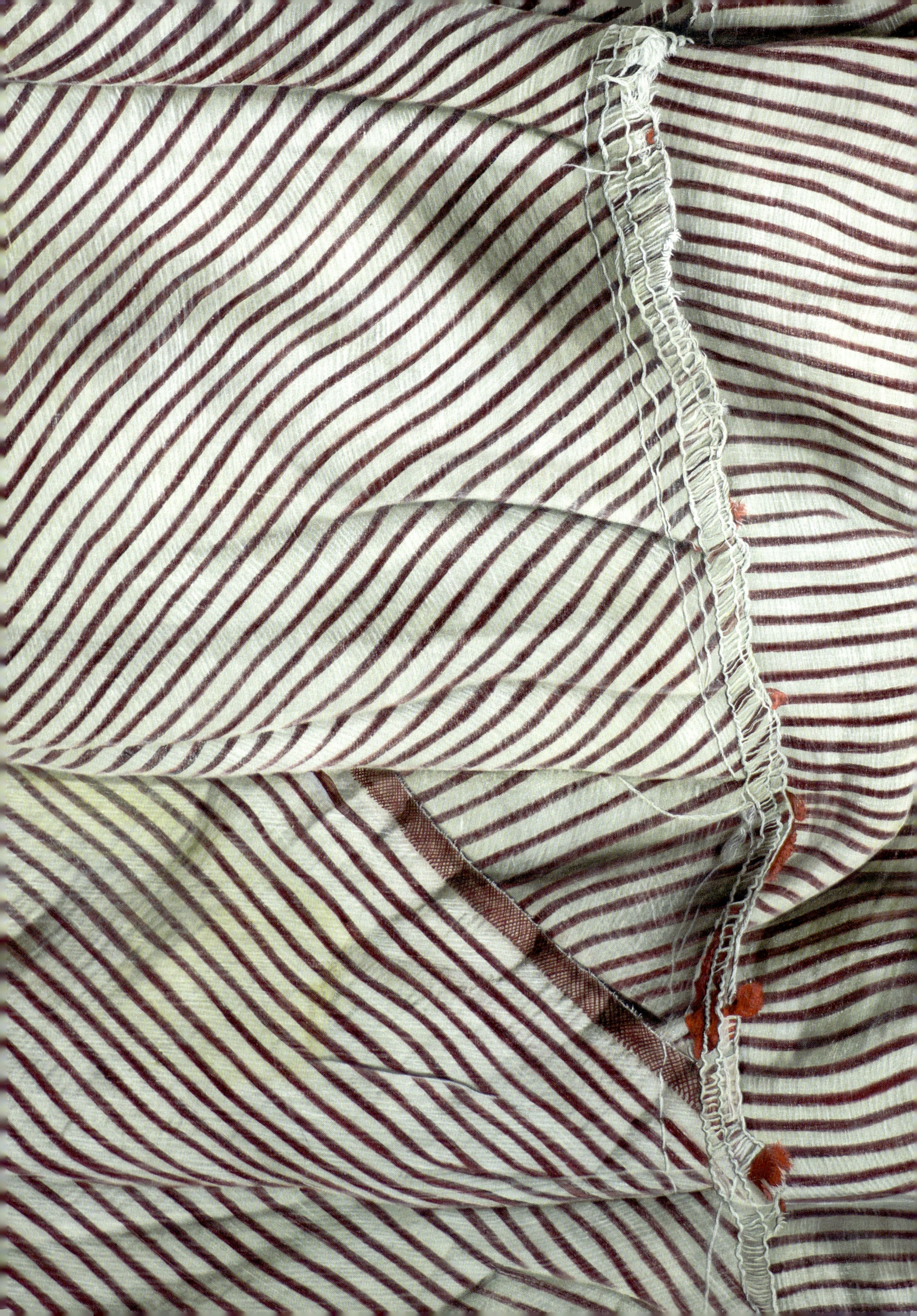

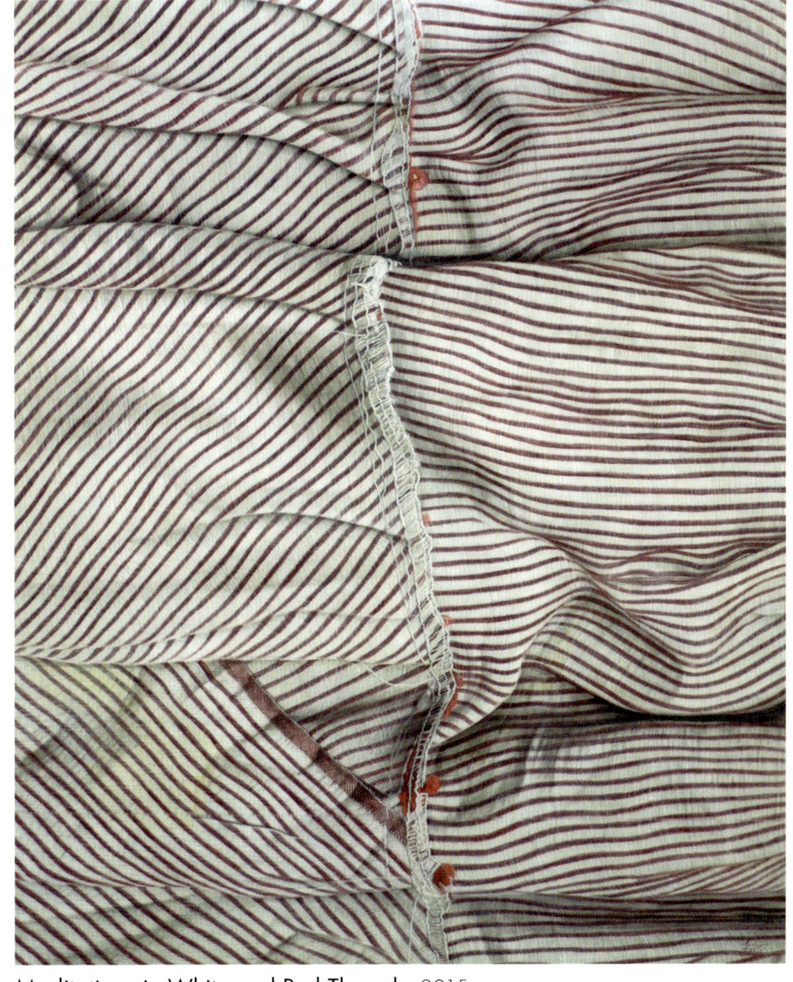

Meditations in White and Red Threads, 2015

Vermillion with White Under, 2015

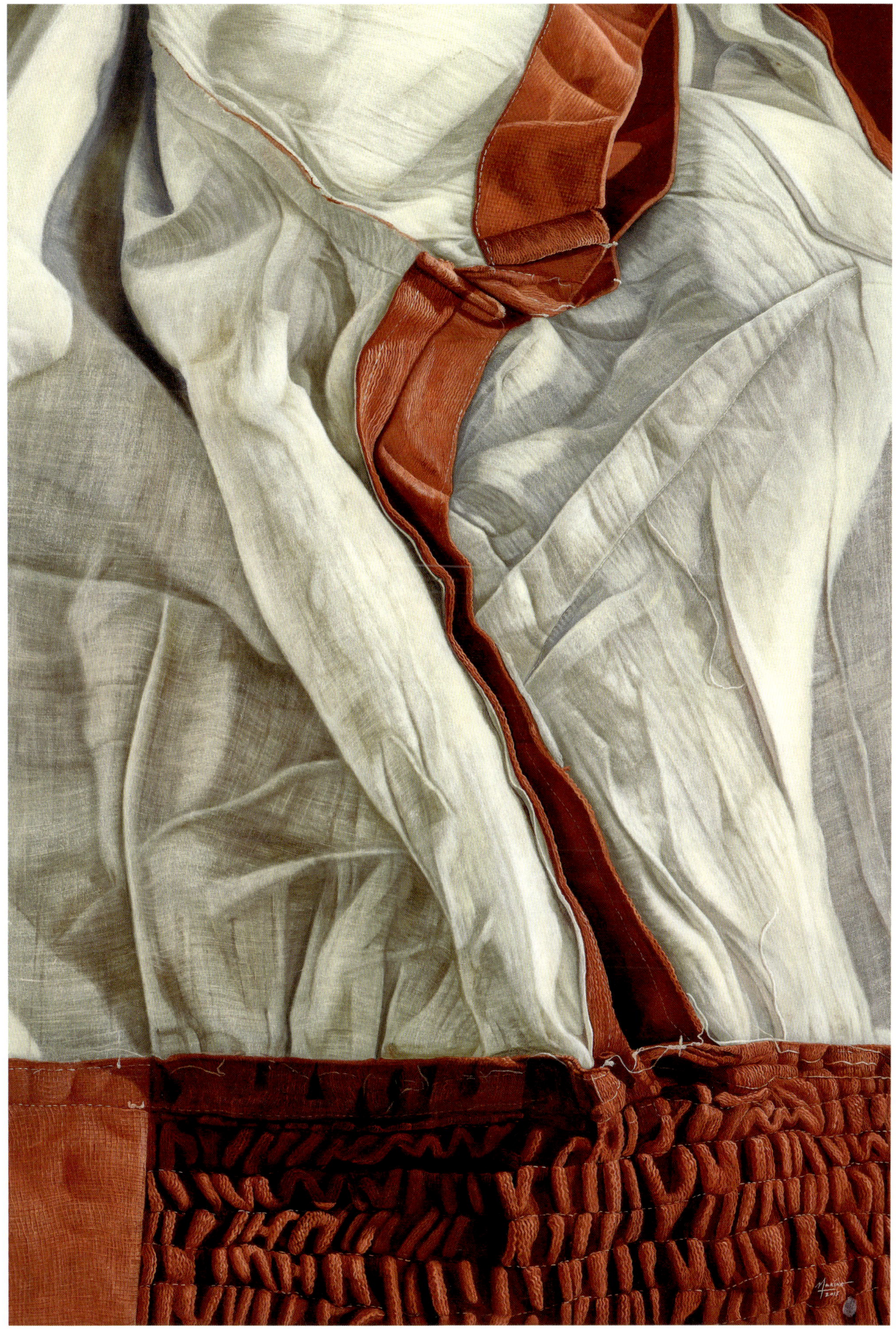

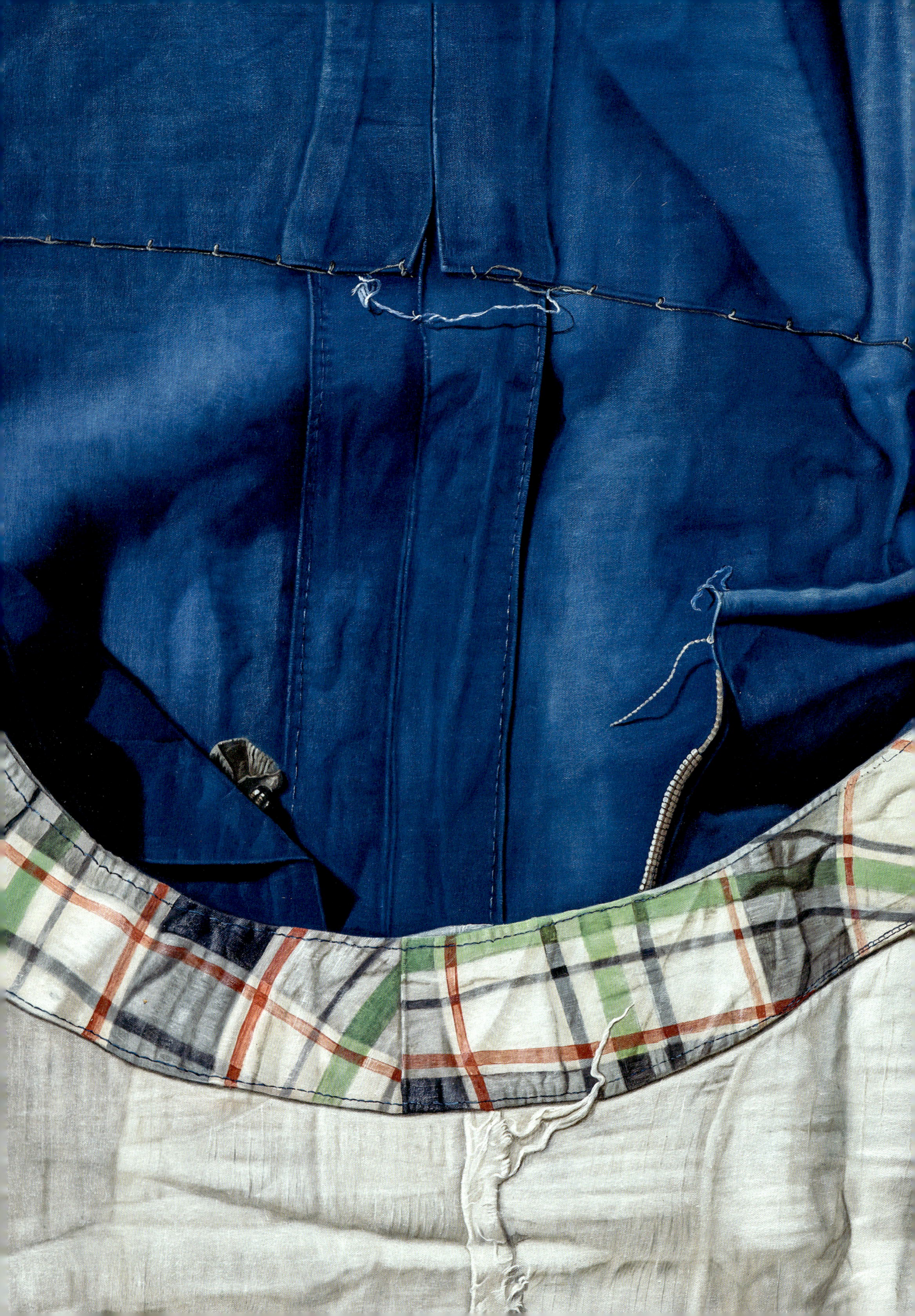

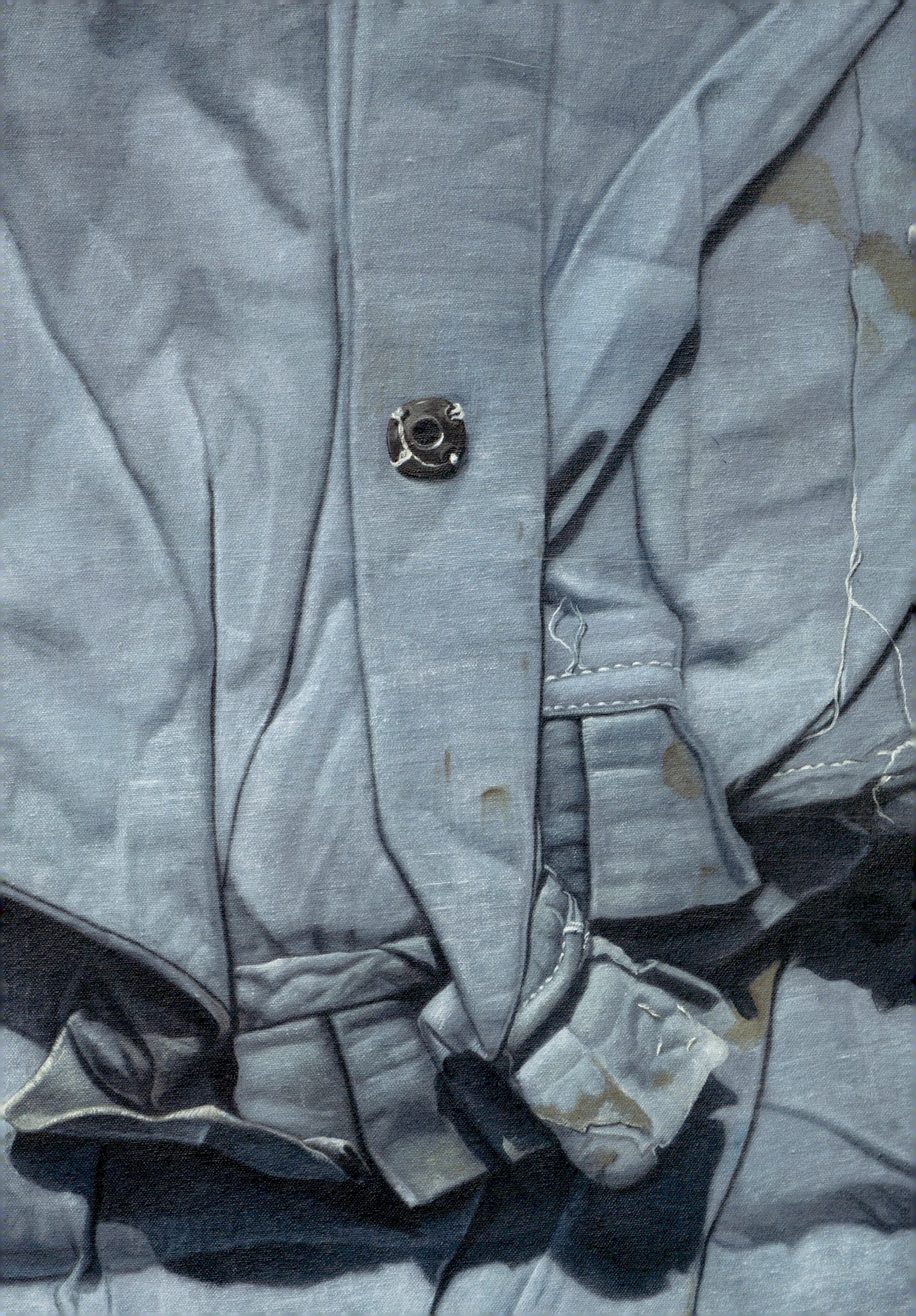

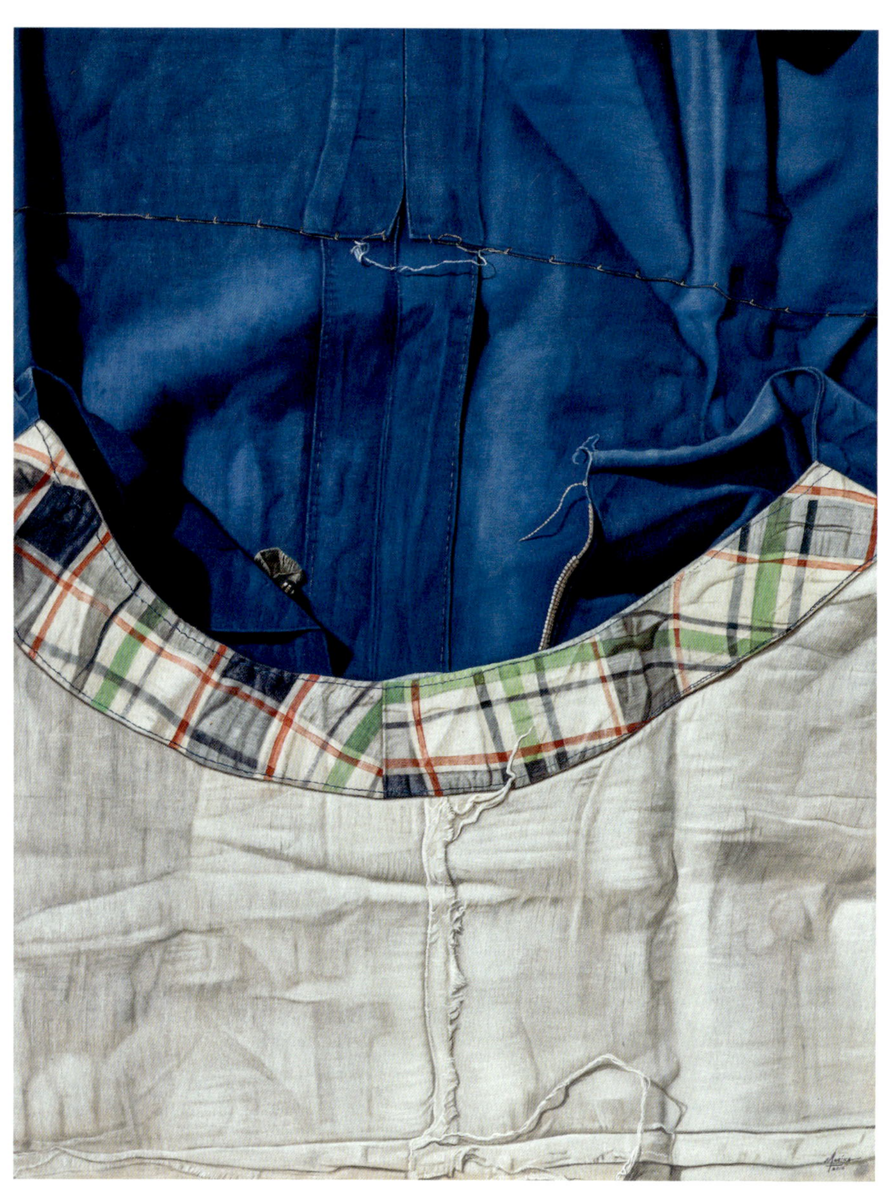

Rainbow Reflections on Blue and White, 2016

Plain with Stains, 2016

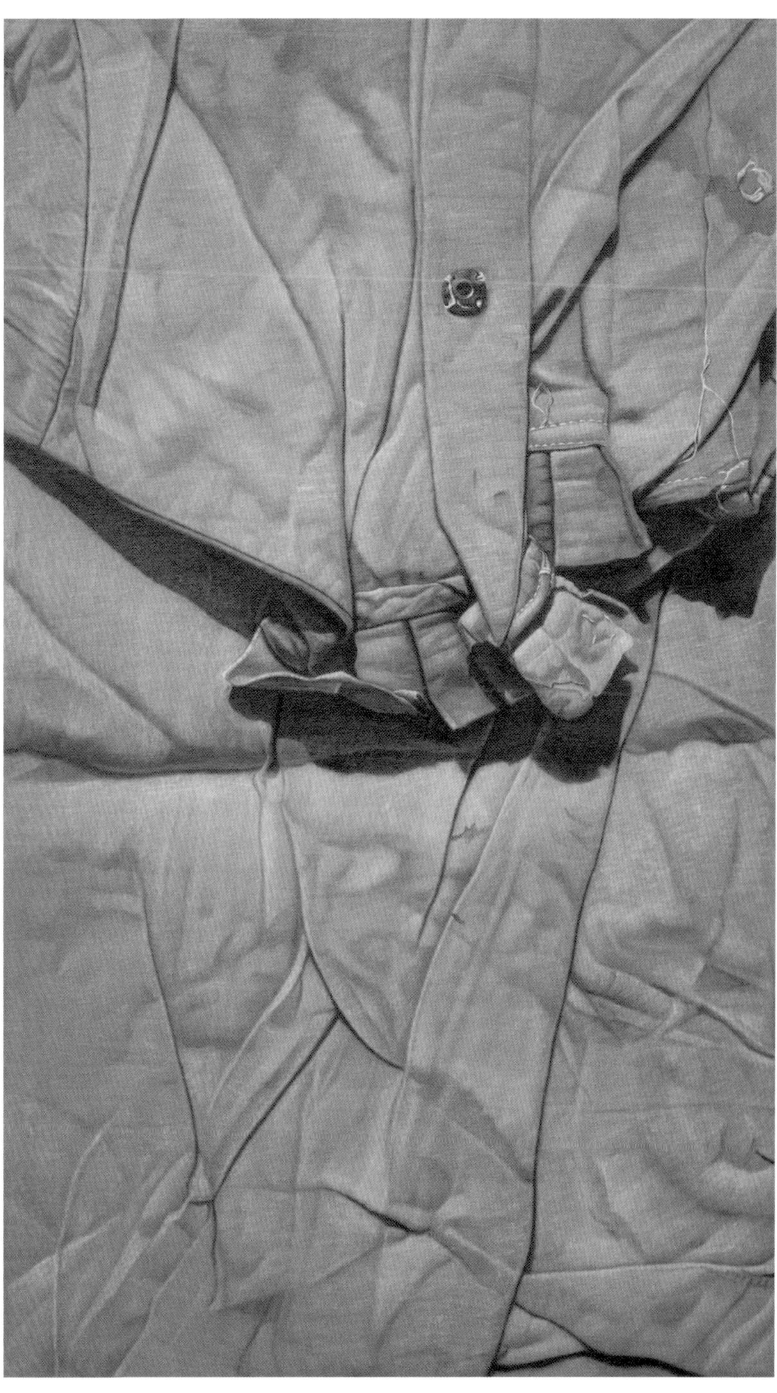

Blue and White with Rickrack, 2016

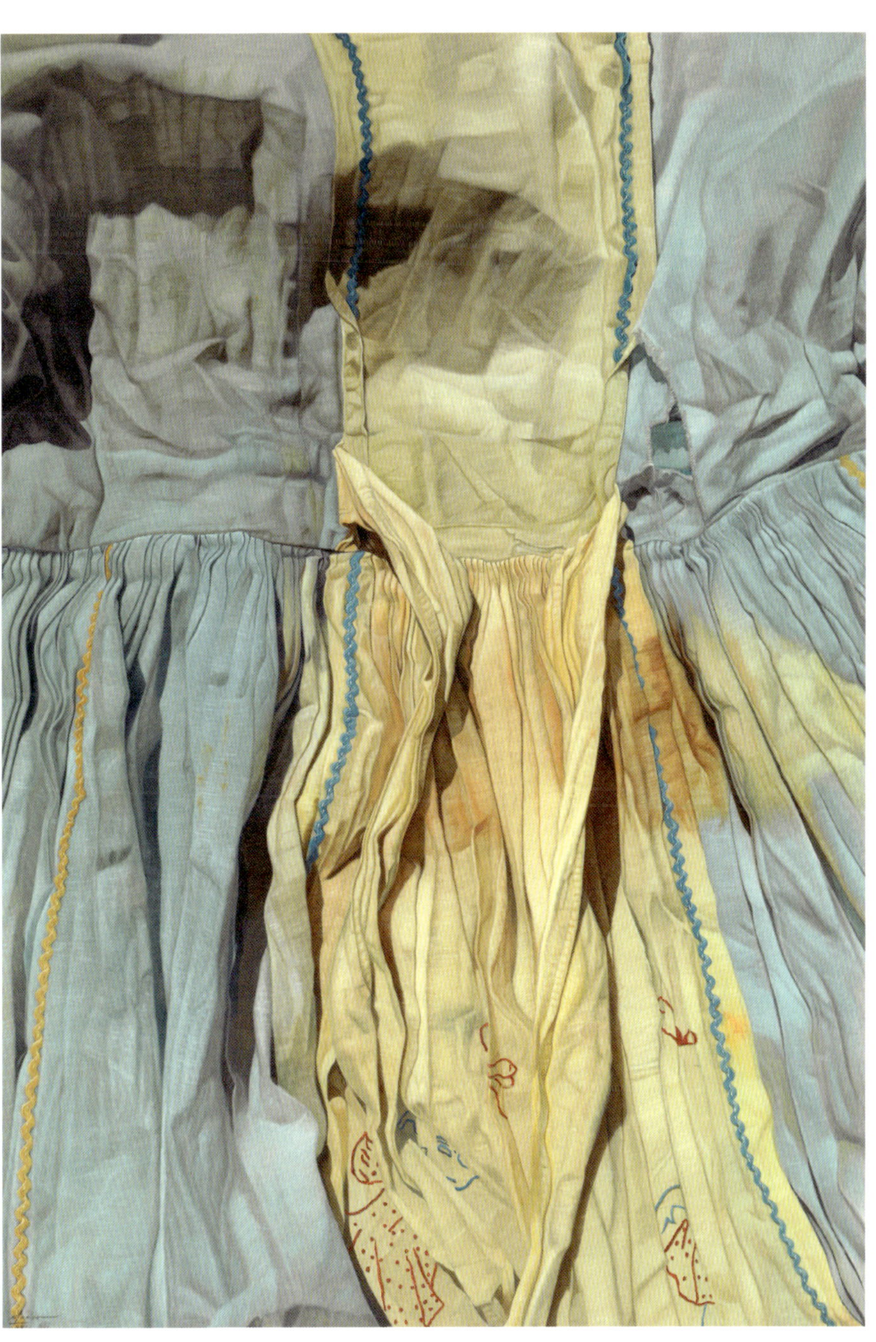

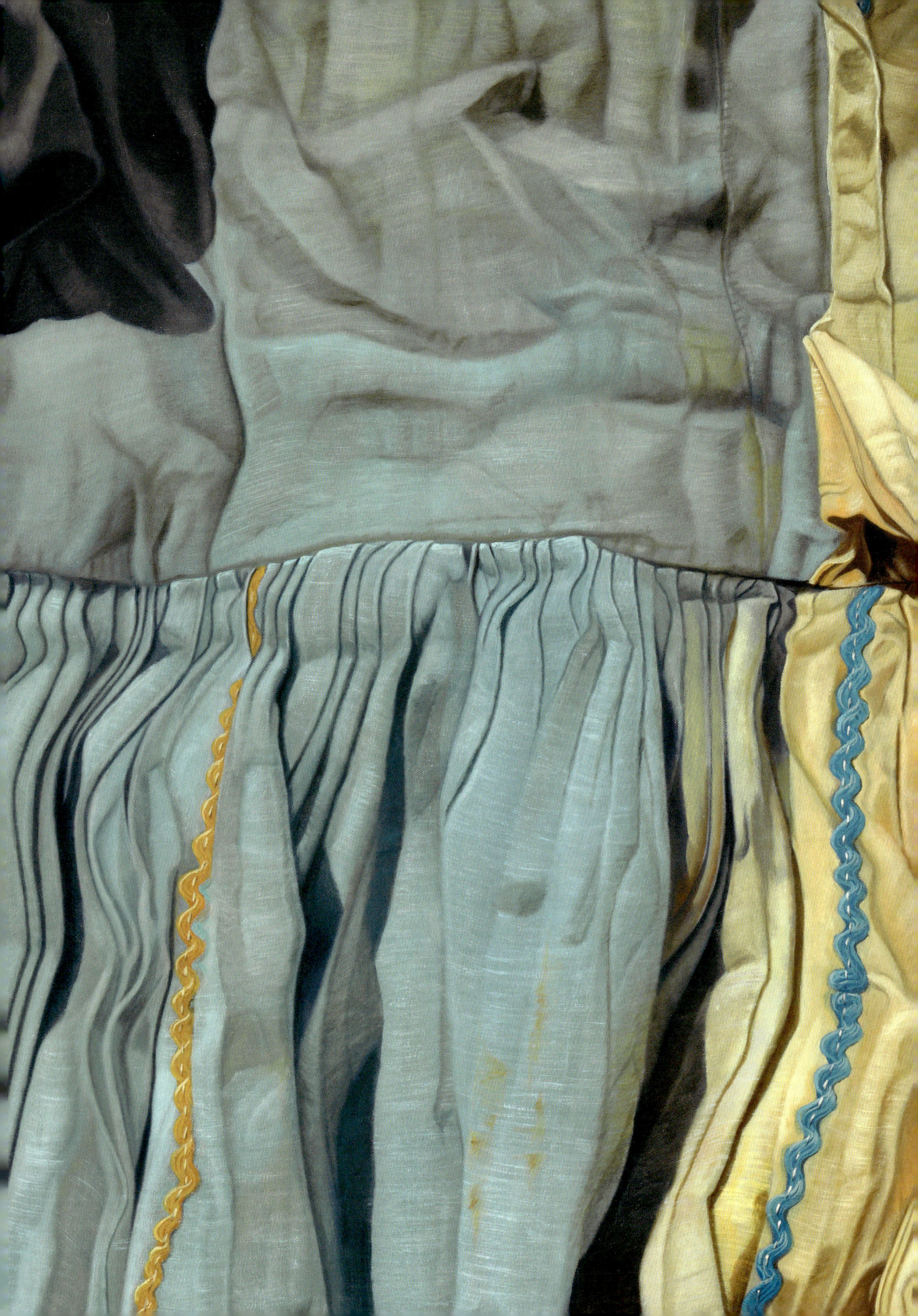

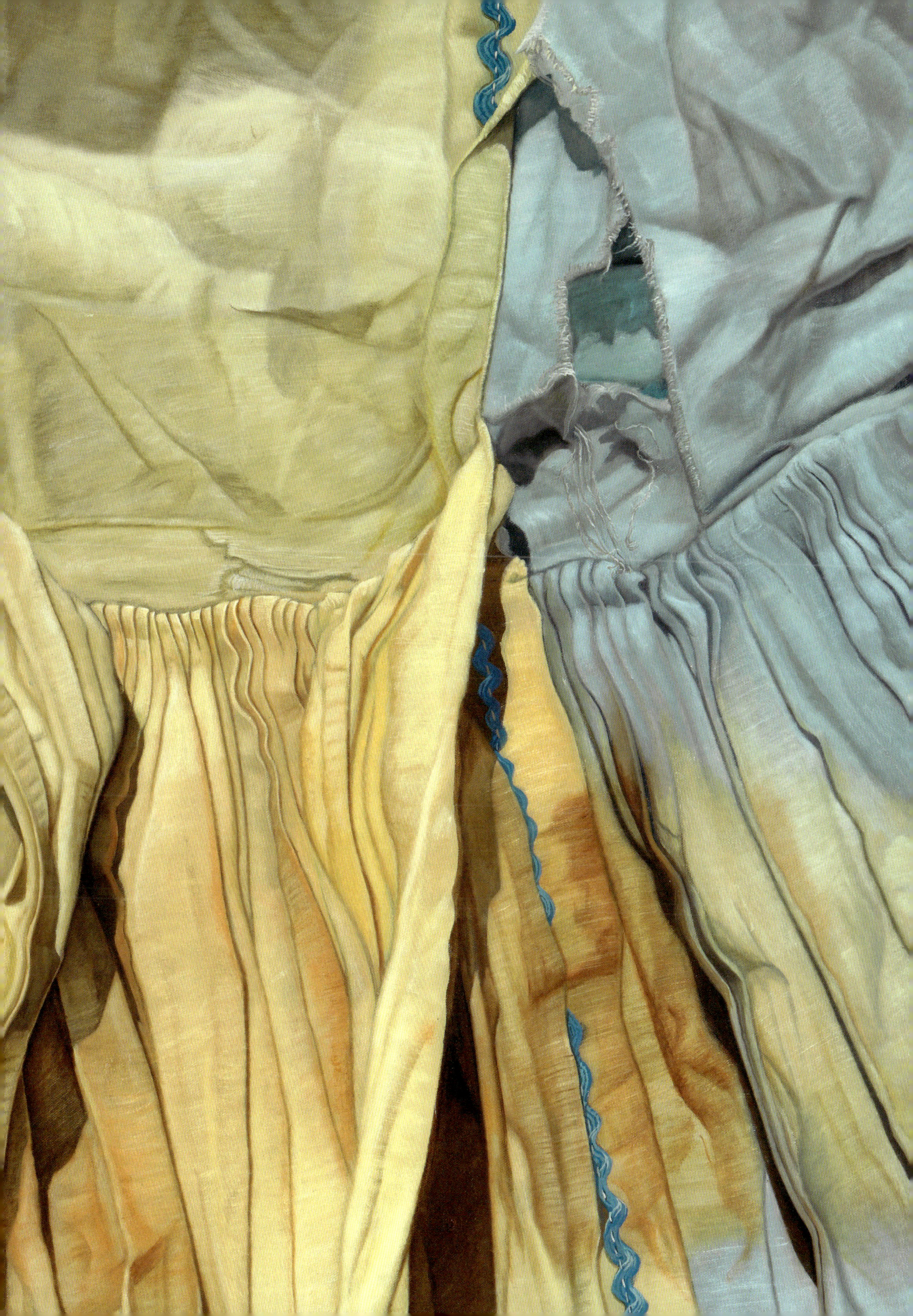

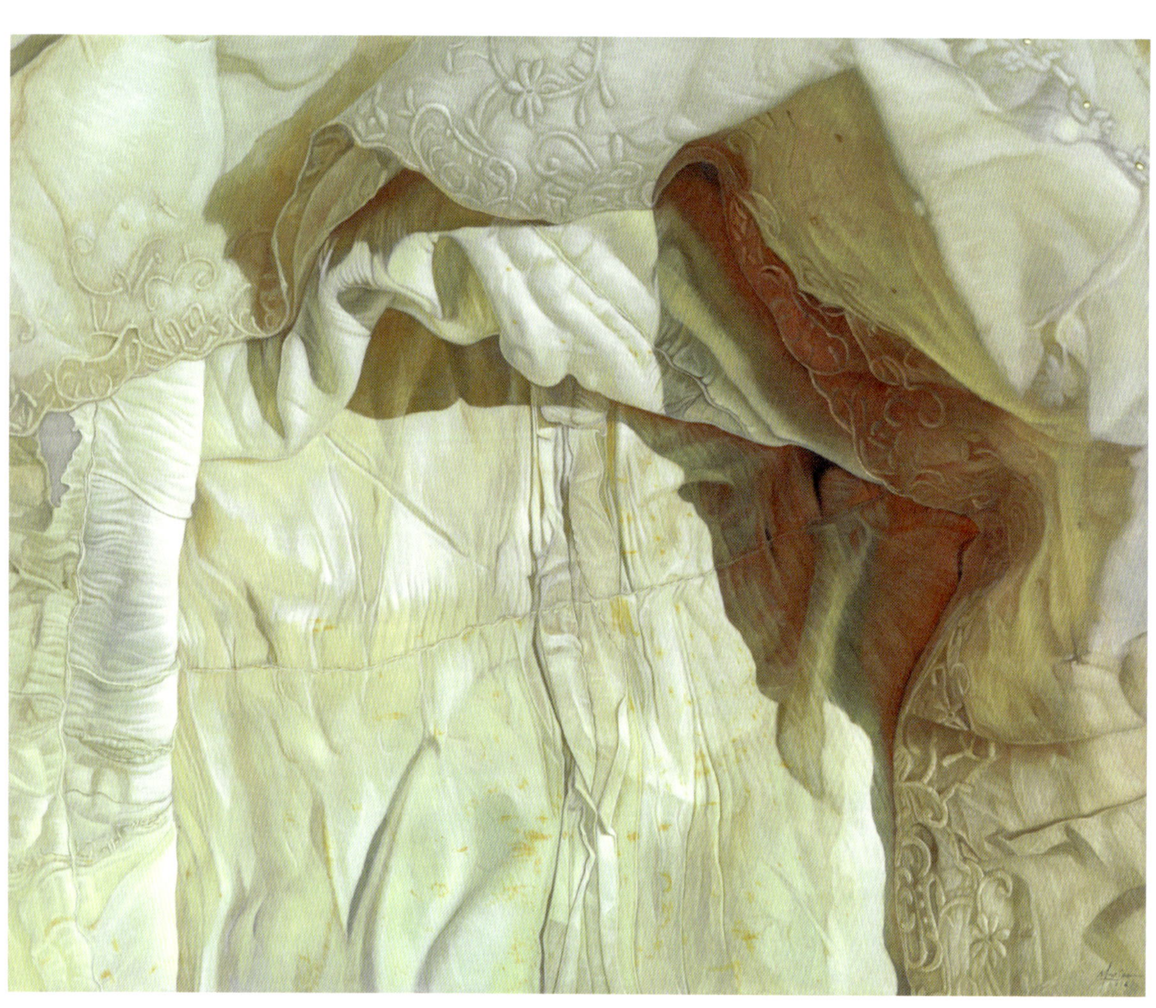

White on White of Laces and Linings Burning Shadows, 2016

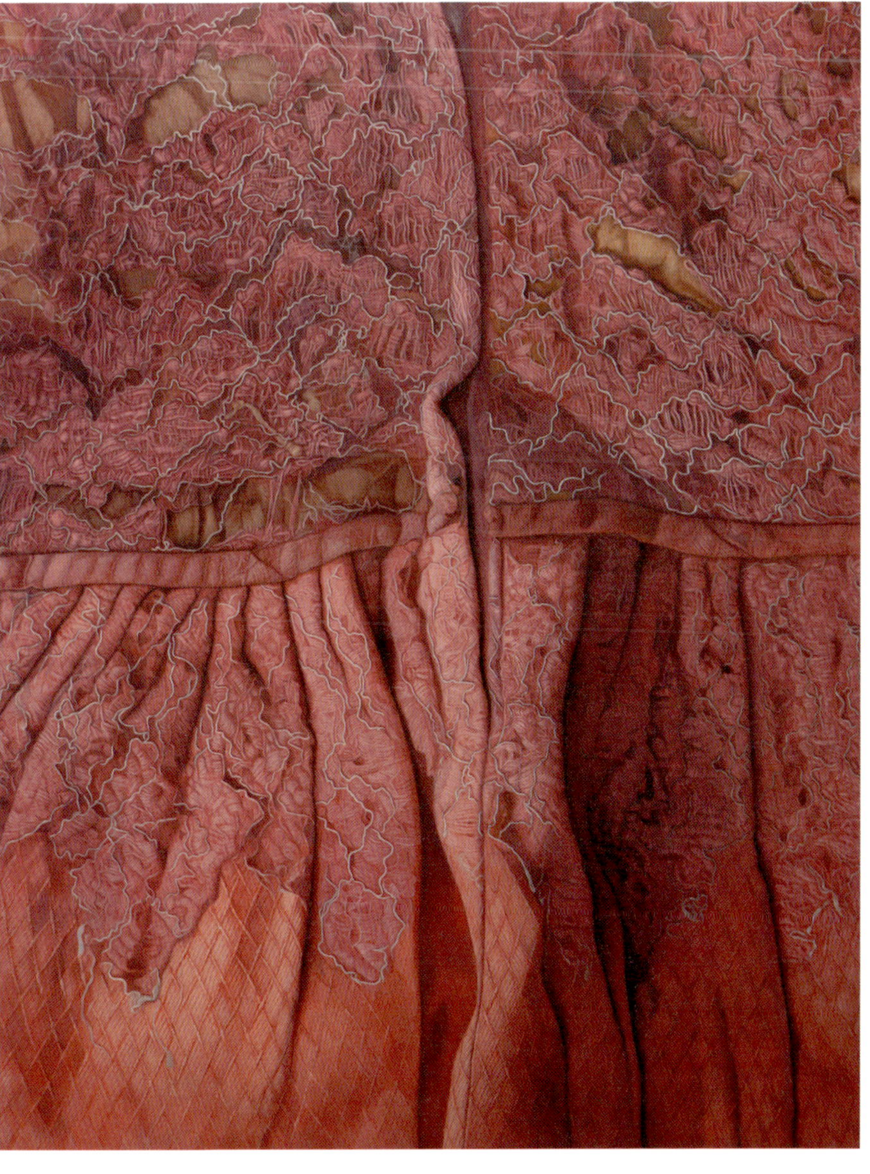

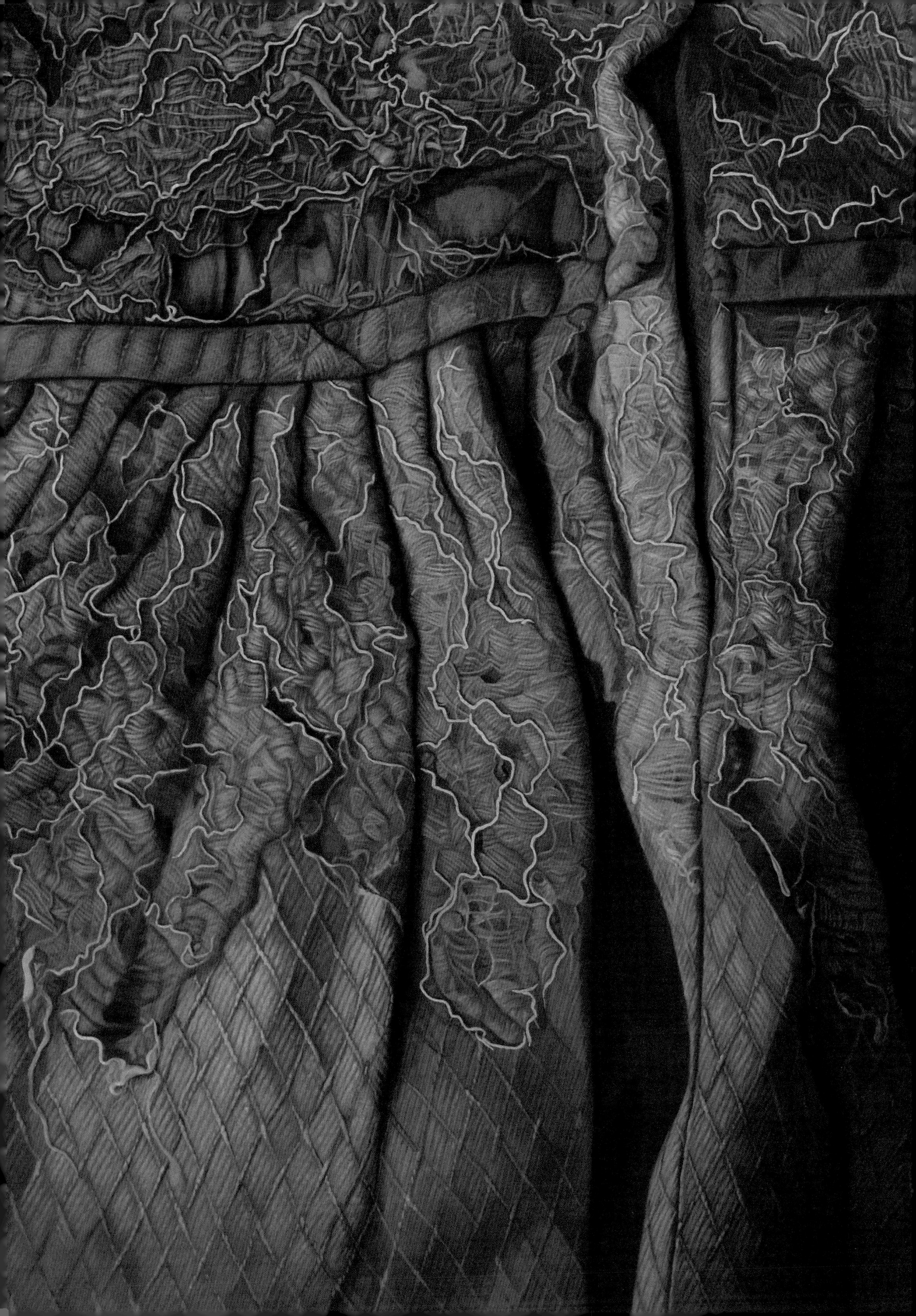

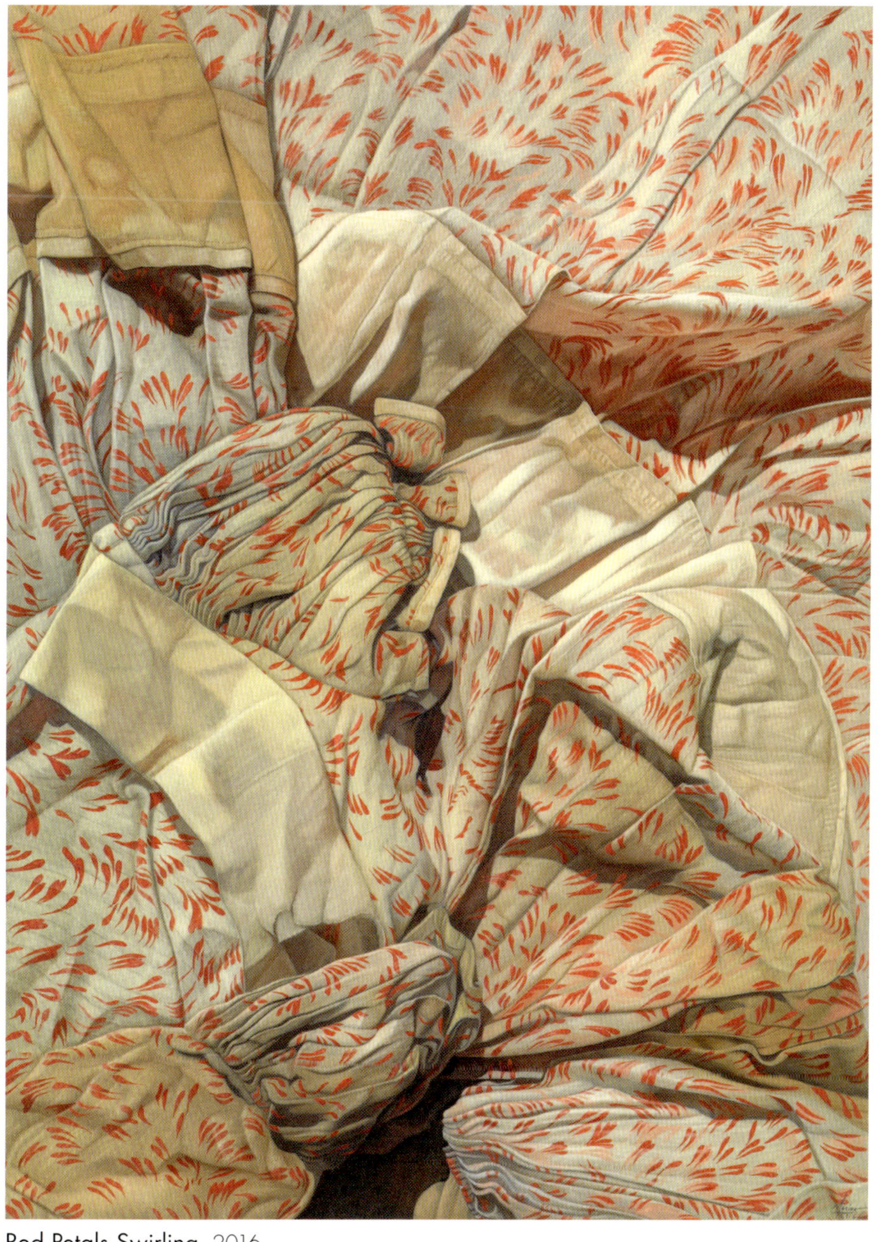

Red Petals Swirling, 2016

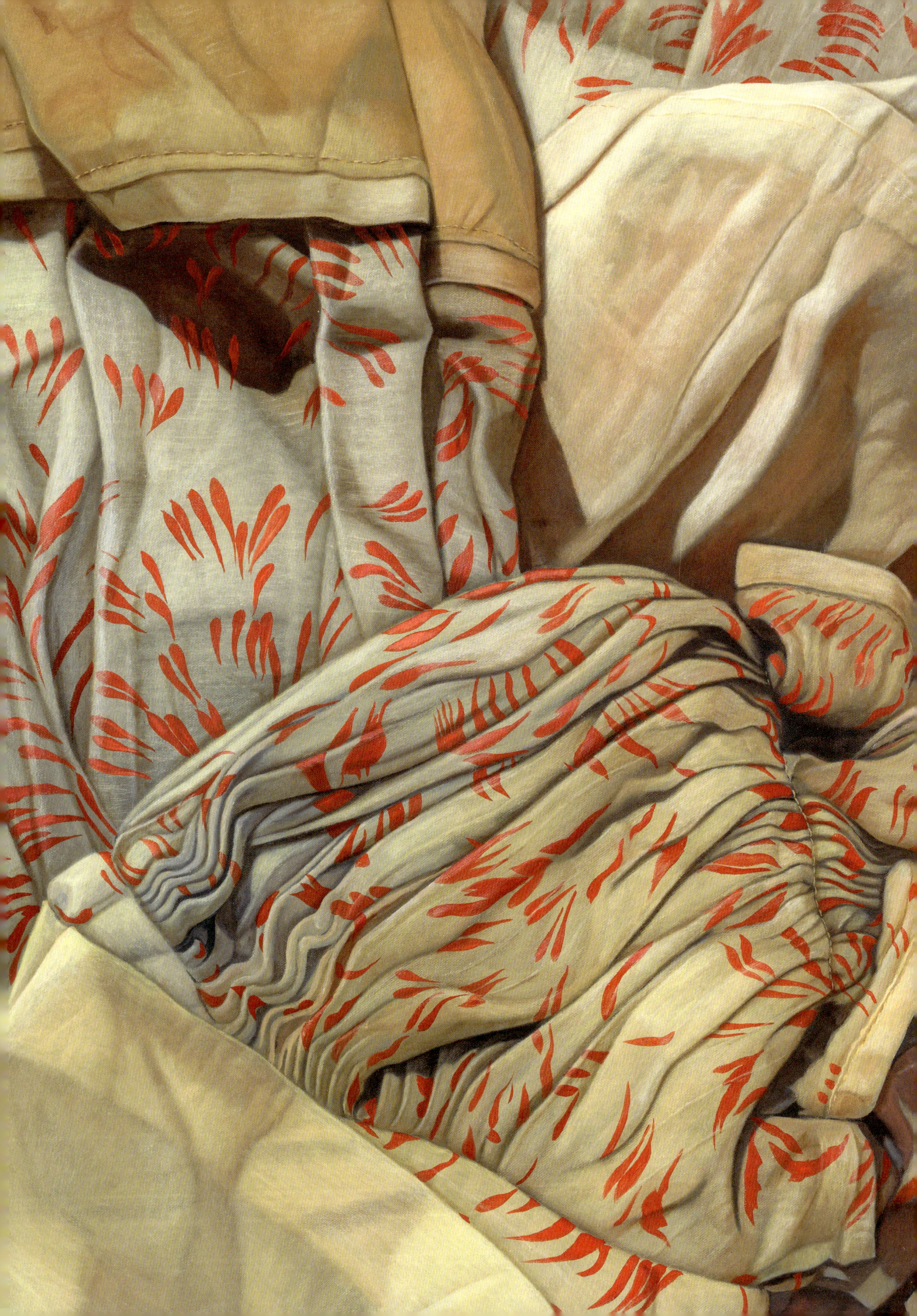

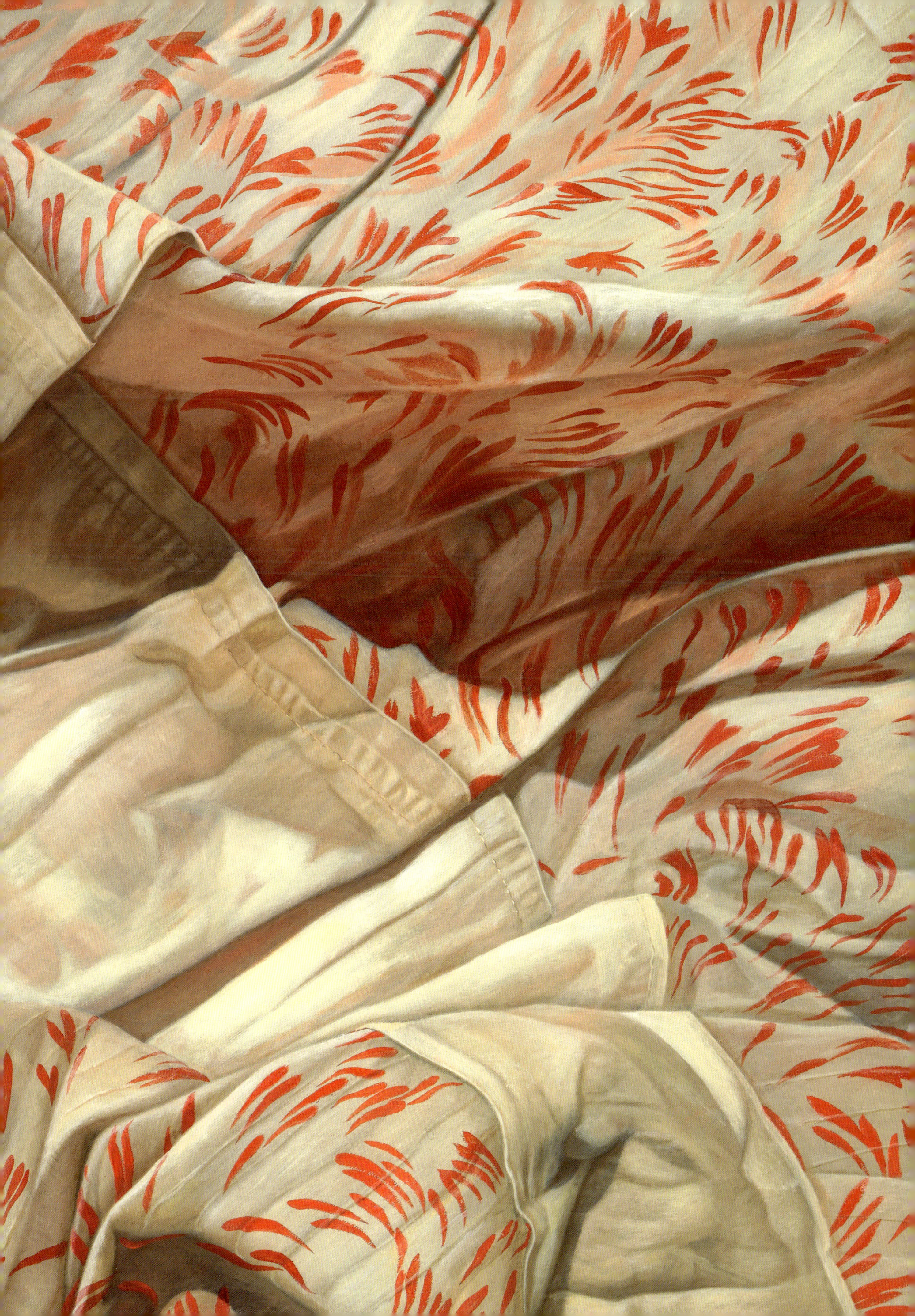

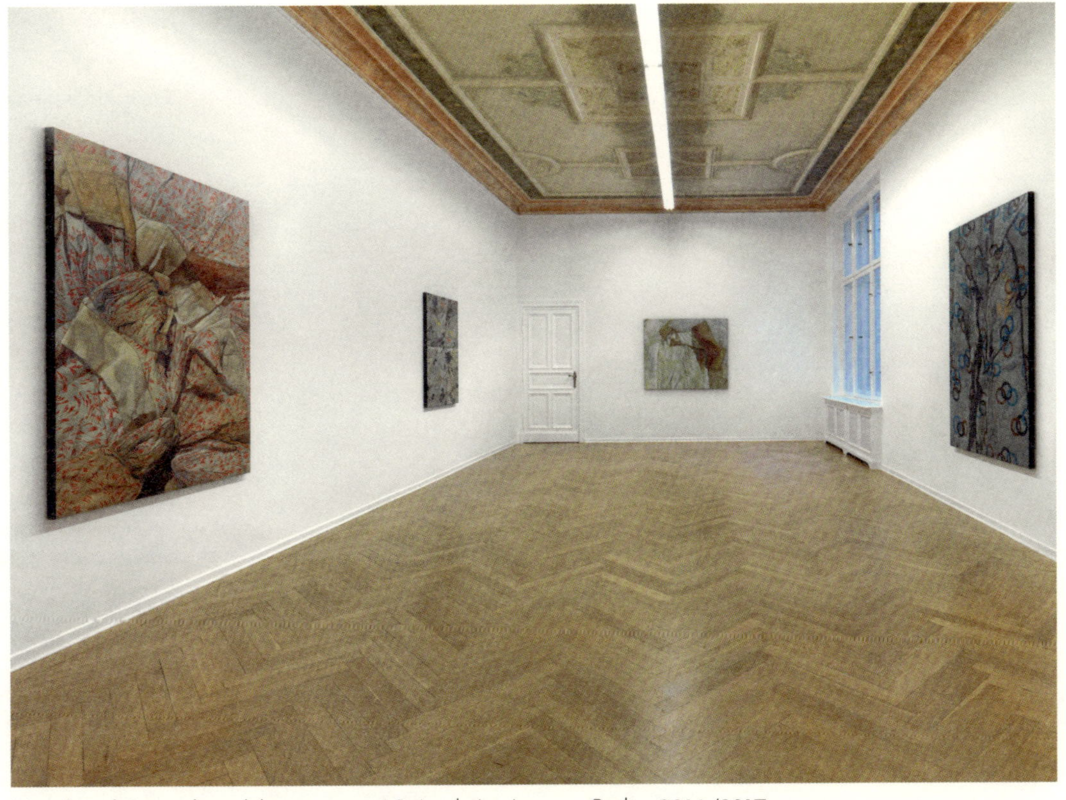

Mend and Amends, exhibition view, A3 Arndt Art Agency, Berlin, 2016/2017

Marina Cruz

1982 Born in Bulacan, Philippines
Lives and works in Bulacan, Philippines

Education

2003 Bachelor of Fine Arts, Major in Painting, University of the Philippines Diliman, Quezon City, Philippines

Selected Solo Exhibitions

2016 **Mend and Amends**, A3 Arndt Art Agency, Berlin, Germany
Memory of the Mundane, Deutsche Knowledge Services (DKS) Appreciating Art in Deutsche Bank Exhibition, BGC Arts Center, Taguig City, Philippines

2015 **Loose Threads**, 1335 Mabini, Manila, Philippines
Wear and Tear, Mind Set Art Center, Taipei, Taiwan
Meditations on Unearthed Terrain, West Gallery, Quezon City, Philippines

2014 **Fabric Skin**, Artinformal, Mandaluyong City, Philippines

2013 **Flower Arrangements**, Finale Art File, Makati City, Philippines
Lost Finds, Artesan Gallery + Studio, Raffles Arcade, Singapore

2012 **Corners of My Sleep**, Artinformal, Mandaluyong City, Philippines
In the House of Memory, Mind Set Art Center, Taipei, Taiwan
Inside Out, BenCab Museum, Baguio City, Philippines

2010 **Simple Depictions** (with Rodel Tapaya), Total Gallery, Alliance Française de Manille, Makati City, Philippines

2011 **Forget Me Not**, West Gallery, Quezon City, Philippines
The Connective Thread, Ernst & Young Building, Singapore

2009 **Spontaneous Moments**, The Drawing Room, Makati, Philippines
Un/Fold, Ateneo Art Gallery, Quezon City, Philippines

2008 **Open House**, The Drawing Room, Makati City, Philippines
Embroidered Landscapes, La Trobe University Visual Arts Center, Bendigo, Victoria, Australia
Lest You Forget, Boston Gallery, Quezon City, Philippines
Recollections, Artinformal, Mandaluyong City, Philippines

2007 **Dollhouse**, Artinformal, Mandaluyong City, Philippines

2005 **Kambal**, Boston Gallery, Quezon City, Philippines

Selected Group Exhibitions

2017 **Passion and Procession: Art of the Philippines**, Art Gallery of New South Wales, Sydney
Pauses of Possibilities, Lopez Museum, Pasig City, Philippines

2016 **Every Island from Sea to Sea: Recent Philippine Art**, Mind Set Art Center, Taipei, Taiwan
Chimères: Visions of South East Asia, Asia Now, Paris Asian Art Fair, France
The Road Not Taken, Mind Set Art Center, Taipei, Taiwan
Forget-Me-Not: Artistic Approaches to Oblivion, Galerie Zimmermann Kratochwill, Graz, Austria

2015 **Wasak! Filipino Art Today**, Arndt Berlin, Germany

2014 **Woman-Home: In the Name of Asian Female Artists**, Kaohsiung Museum of Fine Arts, Taiwan

2013 **The Philippine Contemporary: To Scale the Past and the Possible**, Metropolitan Museum of Manila, Philippines

2011 **BISA: Potent Presences**, Metropolitan Museum of Manila, Philippines

2009 **Daloy: A Continuing Vision of a Center**, Cultural Center of the Philippines, Pasay City, Philippines

2008 **Sentimental Value**, SOKA Contemporary Space and The Drawing Room, Beijing
Strange Familiarities, Familiar Strangers, Alliance Française de Manille, Makati City, Philippines

2007 **Sungdu-an 4: Extensions**, Capitol University Museum of Three Cultures, Cagayan de Oro City, Philippines
Tampo Lapuk, 2nd Dumaguete Terracotta Biennial, Philippines

2006 **A/P: Analogue Playground**, Ateneo Art Gallery, Quezon City, Philippines

2005 **Armour**, Corredor Gallery, College of Fine Arts, University of the Philippines Diliman, Quezon City, Philippines

2004 **Babaylan@Kasibulan.net**, Cultural Center of the Philippines, Pasay City, Philippines
Gamit, UP Vargas Museum, Quezon City, Philippines

2003 **Buod: Celebration of the Year of the Family**, National Commission for Culture and the Arts, Manila, Philippines

2002 **Toys**, Ayala Museum, Makati City, Philippines

Selected Awards

2012 **Thirteen Artists Award**, Cultural Center of the Philippines

2008 **Philippine Art Awards: Grand Prize Ateneo Art Awards**, Philippines

2004 **GSIS Painting Competition**, Philippines: Jurors' Choice

Selected Bibliography

2016 **Flores, Patrick. Every Island From Sea to Sea**. Exh. Cat. Mind Set Art Center, Taipei.
Arndt, Matthias, ed. **Wasak! Filippino Art Today**. Berlin.

2015 Mind Set Art Center, ed. Marina Cruz. Taipei.

2014 **Marina Cruz: Dolled Up**. Exh. pamphlet. Art Fair Philippines. Makati City.
Marina Cruz: Flower Arrangements. Exh. pamphlet. Finale Art File. Makati City.
Ito, Lisa. "Deconstructing dress: Form and history in Marina Cruz's Fabric Skin," in **Marina Cruz: Fabric Skin**. Exh. cat. Artinformal, Mandaluyong City. San Juan.

2013 **Lost Finds: New Works by Marina Cruz**. Exh. cat. Artesan Gallery + Studio. Singapore.
Guazon, Tessa Maria. "Parallel Bounties: Objects as Presense and Phantom in the works of Pamela Yan and Marina Cruz," in **Art Basel Hong Kong: The Art Show**. Exh. cat. Ostfildern.

2012 **Marina Cruz-Garcia: In the House of Memory**. Exh. cat. Mind Set Art Center. Taipei.
Marina Cruz: Inside Out. Exh. cat. BenCab Museum, Baguio City. Quezon City.
Cobangbang, Lena. "Marina Cruz," in **2012 Thirteen Artists Awards**. Exh. cat. CCP – Cultural Center of the Philippines. Pasay City.
Flores, Patrick. "Striking Likeness," in **Imaging Identity: 100 Filipino Self-Portraits. A Selection from the Paulino Que Collection**. Exh. cat. Finale Art File. Makati City.

2011 **Marina Cruz: Forget Me Not**. Exh. pamphlet. West Gallery. Quezon City.

2010 Hilario, Riel. "Marina Cruz," in **Without Walls: A Tour of Philippine Paintings at the Turn of the Millenium.** Edited by Francis Francisco and Maria Chittyrene C. Labiran. Pasig City.

2009 Flores, Patrick. "Home is Leaving," in **Marina Cruz: Home is the place you will leave**. Exh. cat. The Drawing Room. Makati City.

List of Works

pp. 1 and 8 **White Patterns on Red**, 2015
Oil on canvas
157.5 × 127 cm
Anton Mendoza Collection, Philippines

pp. 2/3 and 80 **White on White of Laces and Linings Burning Shadows**, 2016
Oil on canvas
134.6 × 114.3 cm
Teresa O. Reyes Collection, Philippines

pp. 4 and 9 **Faded Green and White Clover**, 2015
Oil on canvas
167.6 × 114.3 cm
Private collection, Italy

p. 7 **Chequered**, 2014
Oil on canvas 152.4 × 114 cm
Mark Tsai Collection, Taiwan

pp. 10–11 **Whites and Blues Torn and Mended by Dragonflies**, 2016
Oil on canvas
121.9 × 91.4 cm
Private collection, Berlin

p. 13 **Stains and Shadows**, 2014
Oil on canvas
153.5 × 101.8 cm
Yi-Wei Hsu Collection

p. 15 **Red and White Stripes**, 2014
Oil on canvas
153.5 × 101.8 cm
Bo-Wen Chen Collection, Taiwan

pp. 16–17 **Blue and White with Pink Under**, 2015
Oil on canvas
121.9 × 101.6 cm
Juan Tseng Hsiang Collection, Taiwan

p. 19 **White Lines on Red Horizontals**, 2015
Oil on canvas
114.5 × 101.6 cm
Private collection, Taiwan

pp. 20 and 23 **Stains and Spots**, 2015
Oil on canvas
157.5 × 132 cm
Sandy Uy Collection, Philippines

pp. 21 and 22 **White on Red with Threads**, 2015
Oil on canvas
135.9 × 101.6 cm
Private collection

p. 25 **Geometric Landscapes**, 2016
Oil on canvas
114 × 152 cm
Private collection

pp. 26–27 **Broken White Threads on Red**, 2015
Oil on canvas
152.4 × 114.9 cm
Private collection, Taiwan

p. 29 **Orange Flowers**, 2015
Oil on canvas
149.9 × 101.6 cm
Private collection, Taiwan

pp. 30/31 **Edilberta's Embroidered Blossoms**, 2015
Oil on canvas
Diptych 81.3 × 171.7 cm
Private collection, Philippines

pp. 32–33 **Nesting Patterns**, 2017
Oil on canvas
221 × 180.3 cm

p. 34 **Security Blanket**, 2015
Embroidery and oil on canvas
92 × 71.1 cm
Private collection, Philippines

p. 35 **Flight and Plight**, 2015
Embroidery and oil on canvas
91.5 × 80.3 cm
Private collection, Philippines

p. 36 **Lost Thoughts**, 2015
Embroidery and oil on canvas
92 × 73.7 cm
Private collection, Philippines

p. 37 **Skies and River**, 2015
Embroidery and oil on canvas
86.6 × 68.8 cm
Private collection, Philippines

pp. 38–39 **Mountainous Terrains**, 2015
Embroidery and oil on canvas
86.6 × 76.8 cm
Private collection, Philippines

p. 41 **Flesh Underneath**, 2017
Oil on canvas
183 × 122 cm
SEACO Collection

pp. 42/43 and 45 **Mend Me**, 2016
Oil on canvas
190 × 200 cm
The Bate Collection, Philippines

pp. 46–47 **When Sonia Was Four (1958)**, 2017
Oil on canvas
261 × 191 cm

p. 48 **Meditations on White and Yellow Against Black**, 2015
Oil on canvas
114.3 × 91.44 cm
Private collection, Philippines

p. 49 **Gregorio's Miniature Cabinet**, 2008
Wood
25.4 × 22.86 × 7.62 cm
Collection of the artist

p. 56 **Pink Crib and Pink Cabinets**, 2017
Oil on canvas
183 × 244 cm

p. 57 **Personal Archive I and II**, 2017
Oil on canvas
183 × 244 cm

pp. 61–63 **Just balls, and atoms, and planets, and a hole**, 2015
Oil on canvas
101.6 × 152.4 cm
Raymond Alfonso Collection, Philippines

p. 65 **Intertwining Rings and Threads**, 2016
Oil on canvas
182.9 × 121.9 cm

p. 67 **Blue Mountain Against White Skies**, 2016
Oil on canvas
122 × 91.4 cm
Private collection

pp. 68–69 **Meditations in White and Red Threads**, 2015
152.4 × 122 cm
Private collection, Philippines

p. 71 **Vermillion with White Under**, 2015
Oil on canvas
152.4 × 101.6 cm
Private collection, Taiwan

pp. 72 and 74 **Rainbow Reflections on Blue and White**, 2016
Oil on canvas
122 × 91.4 cm

pp. 73 and 75 **Plain with Stains**, 2016
Oil on canvas
106.7 × 61 cm
Luis Paolo Pineda Collection, Philippines

pp. 77–79 **Blue and White with Rickrack**, 2016
Oil on canvas
182.9 × 121.9 cm
Dondi and Liza Santos Collection, Philippines

pp. 81–82 **Blush Fibers and Bed Sores**, 2017
Oil on canvas
182.9 × 243.8 cm

pp. 85–87 **Red Petals Swirling**, 2016
Oil on canvas
172 × 121.9 cm
Adela Go Co Collection, Philippines

Photo Credits

As well as the following named individuals, galleries or agencies all images also courtesy of the artist. If not otherwise stated, all photographs taken by the artist.

pp. 1, 8 courtesy of Anton Mendoza Collection
pp. 2/3, 80 courtesy of Teresa O. Reyes Collection, Philippines, and A3 Arndt Art Agency
photo: Bernd Borchardt
pp. 4, 9 courtesy of private collection, Italy and Mind Set Art Center, Taipei
photo: Mind Set Art Center, Taipei
p. 7 courtesy of Mark Tsai Collection, Taiwan, and Mind Set Art Center, Taipei
photo: Mind Set Art Center, Taipei
pp. 10–11 courtesy of private collection, Berlin, and A3 Arndt Art Agency
photo: Bernd Borchardt
p. 13 courtesy of Yi-Wei Hsu Collection and Mind Set Art Center, Taipei
photo: Mind Set Art Center, Taipei
p. 15 courtesy of Bo-Wen Chen Collection, Taiwan, and Mind Set Art Center, Taipei
photo: Mind Set Art Center, Taipei
pp. 16–17 courtesy of Juan Tseng Hsiang Collection
p. 19 courtesy of private collection, Taiwan
pp. 20, 23 courtesy of Sandy Uy Collection
pp. 21, 22, 25 courtesy of private collection
pp. 26–27, 29 courtesy of private collection, Taiwan, and Mind Set Art Center, Taipei
photo: Mind Set Art Center, Taipei
pp. 30/31 courtesy of private collection, Philippines
pp. 32–33 courtesy of A3 Arndt Art Agency
pp. 34–39 courtesy of private collection, Philippines
p. 41 courtesy of SEACO Collection and A3 Arndt Art Agency
pp. 42/43, 45 courtesy of The Bate Collection, Philippines, and A3 Arndt Art Agency
photo: Bernd Borchardt
pp. 46–47 courtesy of A3 Arndt Art Agency
p. 48 courtesy of private collection, Philippines
pp. 56, 57 courtesy of A3 Arndt Art Agency
pp. 61–63 courtesy of Raymond Alfonso Collection, Philippines, and A3 Arndt Art Agency
photo: Bernd Borchardt
p. 65 courtesy of Maria Linda Santos Collection, Philippines, and A3 Arndt Art Agency
photo: Bernd Borchardt
p. 67 courtesy of private collection and Mind Set Art Center, Taipei
pp. 68–69 courtesy of private collection, Philippines
p. 71 courtesy of private collection, Taiwan, and Mind Set Art Center, Taipei
photo: Mind Set Art Center, Taipei
pp. 72, 74 courtesy of Mind Set Art Center, Taipei
photo: Mind Set Art Center, Taipei
pp. 73, 75 courtesy of Luis Paolo Pineda Collection, Philippines
pp. 77–79 courtesy of Dondi and Liza Santos Collection, Philippines, and A3 Arndt Art Agency
photo: Bernd Borchardt
pp. 81–82 courtesy of A3 Arndt Art Agency
pp. 85–87 courtesy of Adela Go Co Collection, Philippines, and A3 Arndt Art Agency
photo: Bernd Borchardt
p. 89 courtesy of A3 Arndt Art Agency
photo: Bernd Borchardt

Colophon

Editors
Matthias Arndt, Tiffany Wood

Managing Editor and Editing
Kristin Rieber

Texts
Matthias Arndt (foreword)
Philipp Bollmann (interview)
Kira Jürjens (essay)

Design
Delia Keller, Gestaltung Berlin

Translation
Ann Marie Bohan

Copy Editing
Sarah Quigley

Image Editing
max-color, Berlin

Production Management
DISTANZ Verlag, Rebecca Wilton

Production
optimal media GmbH, Röbel/Müritz

Cover Image
Intertwining Rings and Threads (detail), 2016

Distribution
Gestalten, Berlin
www.gestalten.com
sales@gestalten.com

ISBN 978-3-95476-194-4

Printed in Germany

Published by
DISTANZ Verlag
www.distanz.de

Presented by
www.arndtartagency.com

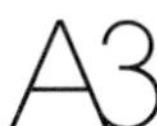

Acknowledgements
Matthias Arndt would like to thank Kristin Rieber and her team for the diligent production, translation, and editing of this book, Delia Keller for the wonderful book design, and Uta Grosenick and her team at DISTANZ Verlag for the ongoing excellent collaboration.